Everyday Phrases

EVERYDAY PHRASES

Their Origins and Meanings

NEIL EWART

GUILD PUBLISHING
LONDON

First published in the U.K. 1983 by Blandford Press

This edition published 1985 by
Book Club Associates
by arrangement with Blandford Press

Reprinted 1986

Distributed in the United States by
Sterling Publishing Co., Inc.
2 Park Avenue, New York, N.Y. 10016

British Library Cataloguing in Publication Data

Ewart, Neil
    Everyday phrases.
1. English language—Etymology
2. English language—Terms and phrases
I. Title
422   PE1571

ISBN 0 7137 1354 2

Typeset in 10/12pt Monophoto Photina
by August Filmsetting, Warrington, Cheshire
Printed and bound in Great Britain by
Biddles Ltd, Guildford and King's Lynn

—

Contents

Introduction

It is almost impossible to get through a day without using, or hearing, some catch phrase of other. Many everyday phrases may appear to be modern, but some have been in existence for a surprisingly long time. They are such an integral part of everyday conversation that we usually accept them without thinking — aware of what they have come to mean but not knowing how they have been derived.

The origins and meanings of over 400 selected phrases in everyday use are here explained in detail. One of the main aims in the research and writing of the book has been to spread the net wide to include as much interesting background material on the phrases as possible, as well as the stories associated with them. Some of these stories may appear incredible, but truth is, after all, stranger than fiction.

Achilles heel When this is used as an everyday expression, it refers to the weak and vulnerable point in something, or in a person's character which is, otherwise, without fault.

It originates from the story of Thetis who held her son Achilles by the heel, when he was a child, and dipped him in the river Styx to make him invulnerable. During the subsequent Trojan wars, in which Achilles distinguished himself as the bravest of fighters, he was finally slain by an arrow directed to the one vulnerable part of his body — the tendon of the heel by which his mother had held him, and which had therefore remained dry, when she had dipped him in the Styx.

To go down the aisle has been used, for many years, to imply getting married. It is a mistaken expression as brides do not walk down the aisle but along the central passage of the church, known as the 'nave'. The aisles are on the left and right of the church, running parallel with the nave.

In the theatre, the phrase 'to have them rolling in the aisles' means that the audience are laughing so uncontrollably at the performance that those near the passageways, or aisles, are almost falling 'in stitches' out of their seats on to the floor.

An albatross around one's neck refers to the guilt one has to bear, which may be with one for a long time, for something one has done wrong.

The albatross is a remarkable sea bird with an 11–14 ft (3–4 m) wingspan, depending on the species, which enables it to sail with and against the wind, without visible wing strokes, for half an hour or more at a time. These birds can circle the globe in eighty days, and this is not uncommon. They make use of the Roaring Forties and other trade winds, only landing on remote oceanic islands to breed. They can live to over thirty years of age, although some are believed to have reached seventy.

According to nautical superstition, it was considered unlucky to kill an albatross as these birds were believed to embody the souls of departed mariners. Coleridge's well-known poem *The Ancient Mariner*, first published in 1798, tells the story of a sailor who kills an albatross. When this brings bad luck to his ship, the dead bird is hung round his neck by his shipmates as a sign of his guilt. Although he repents, and is eventually forgiven, his conscience continues to distress him. The albatross remains with him in spirit, his guilt weighs heavily on him, like a lead weight around his neck, even though he goes from land to land warning others against the cruelty of killing God's creatures.

To wear an Albert An 'Albert' became popular during Victorian times. It was a type of heavy watch-chain which ran across a waistcoat from one pocket to another, through a central vertical buttonhole. Its fame came about when Prince Albert, consort of Queen Victoria, set the fashion, after being presented with a chain of this type by the jewellers of Birmingham, during a visit there, in 1849.

Prince Albert not only popularized the wearing of this watch-chain, but also his own Christian name, although it was Queen Victoria's wish that no future king should be called Albert. When George VI became king he respected her wish, even though his first name was Albert.

All my eye and Betty Martin implies that something is meaningless, utter nonsense, or untrue. 'That's all my eye' is often used today as a shortened version. The origin of the full phrase is said to have arisen from a British sailor's interpretation of *O mihi, beate Martine*, which he misheard in an Italian church when his ship visited a nearby port.

The answer's a lemon originated at the beginning of the 20th century in the USA. The acid-juiced fruit known as the lemon was used to denote a sharp, or sarcastic, reply to a question or request considered unreasonable or ridiculous. It was adopted a few years later in England and taken to mean 'no' or 'nothing doing'.

An apple a day keeps the doctor away is a phrase that has been used for generations which, in more recent times, has been scientifically proved. Tests carried out at Leeds University, in 1981, showed that fewer calls were made on doctors by people who ate a lot of raw apples than those who did not.

The apple tree has been regarded as holy, or magical, since early times and has featured in many Greek, Roman, Norse, and other legends. It is mentioned in the Bible many times. Pliny (23–79 AD), the great writer and historian of ancient Rome, mentions over twenty varieties of apples which were common in his day.

Today, wherever it grows throughout the world — in America,

Europe, or in England, where it was probably introduced by the Romans — the apple has won a health-giving reputation, both for its preventive and curative powers. The fruit provides vitamin C, as well as large amounts of protein, pectin, sugars, numerous mineral salts — including copper, iron and manganese for healthy blood, sodium and potassium — as well as calcium and phosphorus for healthy bones.

Raw apples help to reduce general illness, absenteeism from work, and mental stress — but they should be eaten with the skin and chewed well. Slimmers also welcome raw apples as they contain only 40 calories. However, if the fruit is eaten as an apple-dumpling the calorie count rockets to 340.

To upset the apple cart This phrase is first recorded in use in 1796. It was adapted for everyday use to describe the spoiling of someone's carefully laid plans, or some unexpected intervention which leads to a state of disorder and confusion.

Until the 19th century roads were generally rough and streets were narrow. For country people, the mere act of getting themselves and their goods to market safely over considerable distances was quite an achievement. One can imagine how annoyed they must have been when the carts containing their precious produce were toppled over, particularly if they had perishable items such as apples, which would become damaged when scattered and ruin the hopes of a profitable sale.

In medieval times markets were vital for the selling of produce — but the right to hold them in towns could only be granted by royal charter. As the markets grew the authorities erected elaborate market crosses to give shelter to country people selling their produce. One of the finest still to be seen in Britain is at the junction of the four main roads in the centre of the cathedral city of Chichester in West Sussex.

Approval *see* SEAL of approval

To chance one's arm is to take a risk, in the hope of obtaining some advantage or other, or trusting to luck in doing something that one has never done before. The phrase is of military origin; it referred to anyone who broke the regulations and ran the risk of losing a badge on their arm. An NCO for instance, if caught, might lose a stripe.

Aunt *see* An aunt SALLY

To have an axe to grind is to have a concealed personal interest in a

[11]

matter — a selfish motive which can lead to personal gain or profit.

The phrase comes from a story told by Benjamin Franklin (1706–1790), the American statesman, writer, and scientist. When young he was asked by a man, who admired his father's grindstone, how it worked. As young Franklin showed him, the man positioned his own axe on it and the more the boy turned the wheel, the more he praised him. Then, when the job was finished, he laughed at the boy, and walked off without so much as saying 'thank you'.

Don't throw the baby out with the bath water This expression warns that when you are throwing anything away it is best to make sure you are not disposing of anything vital that you might need later. Alternatively, if pressure is being put on you to change your point of view, don't throw away all your ideas, stick to the ones in which you firmly believe; just make the necessary adjustments that will meet with approval, but do not abandon your ideals or main beliefs.

During World War II, the parachutes used by paratroops undergoing training at an RAF Station were tested periodically with dummies dropped from a captive balloon, similar to those at the end of a wire and winch used in the balloon barrages. When an RAF pilot went up in the basket to experience his first ride in a lighter-than-air-craft, he helped the despatcher off-load six of the parachutes, with their dummies, through the gaping hole in the floor of the basket, and watched all open successfully at the end of their static lines.

As the balloon was about to be lowered to the ground to take on the next test-load, it stuck. It suddenly struck him how foolish the whole exercise had been, for if things went seriously wrong, or the balloon broke away, they had disposed of their only chance of escape with the six parachutes thrown out, as neither of them wore a parachute themselves. In other words they had 'thrown the baby out with the bath water'.

[12]

Back to the drawing board Although the best inventions are often the simplest, none are easy, and long hours, frequently adding up to many years, of relentless work and calculations are necessary before success or perfection is achieved. When things go wrong, it is often necessary to make a fresh start from the beginning and, as most plans and inventions have to be drawn and worked out on paper first, the phrase for starting anything afresh, 'Back to the drawing board', came into general use. It is also applied light-heartedly to some incident, humorous rather than calamatous. For example, when someone jumps off the end of the pier with wings, trying to emulate Daedalus, but fails to become airborne and plunges into the sea, like Icarus, he might resurface with some such remark as, 'Ah well, back to the drawing board.'

BACK TO SQUARE ONE is another phrase which means having to start something from the beginning again, originating from games played on boards having numbered squares, where square one is the start. In early sports commentaries on the radio a game such as football could be followed more easily by referring to a diagram of the pitch, divided into numbered squares, printed in the listeners' radio programmes.

Backroom boys The phrase arose as a result of a speech made by Lord Beaverbrook, in Britain during World War II, when recognizing the valuable contribution made by the scientists, specialists, inventors and researchers who carried out their hard work, without receiving any public praise or recognition. Beaverbrook said: 'To whom must praise be given? I will tell you. It is the boys in the back room. They do not sit in the limelight, but they are the men who do the work.'

Today, backroom boys continue to work behind the scenes in laboratories and elsewhere in industry and still remain anonymous partly because of the secret nature of their work.

To go baldheaded for something or someone, is to pursue a purpose, or person, without restraint and regardless of the consequences.

The phrase arose from an incident during the Battle of Warburg, in 1760, when the hat and wig of the Commander-in-Chief in Germany, the Marquis of Granby, fell off as he was leading a cavalry charge. He was so incensed that he continued to gallop flat out — baldheaded — at the enemy.

The marquis was a brave and brilliant soldier, and generous too. After his campaigns he arranged for many of his wounded and disabled NCOs to be installed as keepers of various inns. This is one reason why so many inns are called 'The Marquis of Granby'.

[13]

To balk someone — A stumbling block — Barring the way

TO BALK SOMEONE is to thwart or hinder them and is similar to the other widely used expression of PUTTING A STUMBLING BLOCK IN THEIR WAY, or bringing about some circumstance that will cause them difficulty. Both expressions, when used today, really mean to impede someone's actions, prevent them from carrying them out properly, or to hinder them in some way. The 'stumbling block' is mentioned in the Bible in Romans 14:13 '. . . that no man put a stumbling block or an occasion to fall in his brother's way'.

Originally, the 'balk' referred to a timber beam which could be placed across a door on the inside to prevent any intruder from entering. Some ancient houses, and others renovated to look like old ones, have wooden hinged or sliding latches to secure them and a small wooden peg or 'balk', which hung conveniently in place on the end of a leather toggle when not in use, could be used to secure the latch and prevent it from sliding or being lifted by anyone outside.

The use of wooden locks and keys to secure houses and possessions can be traced back 4,000 years; the Romans were the first to use metal ones. In the Middle Ages keys were often 1 ft (0.3048 m) long, and heavy. Castles and larger houses required many keys to secure all the doors, wooden balks found favour through always being conveniently in place, economic to produce, and easy to operate.

Yet another expression, BARRING THE WAY, has the same theme of obstructing a person's progress, plans or actions. This is still observed as an ancient custom at weddings in certain areas of Britain. Departure from the church after the ceremony is barred by a rope, or other object, at the churchyard gate, and not removed until the bridegroom has paid a toll. In some ceremonies the groom lifts his bride over the obstruction, without the need for payment, to ensure good luck.

Having a ball *see* Eat, drink, and be MERRY

When the balloon goes up refers to the start of some big operation and, in particular, to something of great importance which is expected, but with some degree of anxiety. The phrase, which is still used today, was current during both world wars when barrage balloons were raised on wires from winches, both on land and from ships at sea, to protect major targets during air raids. Their purpose was to prevent enemy aircraft from being able to make their attacks from low level, which were likely to be more accurate than those from higher altitudes, and there is no doubt that they played an important role as a deterrent.

[14]

Every plus usually has a minus, though, and barrage balloons were no exception. During the early years of World War II many pilots were still flying aircraft without full navigational aids. They had no radio, radar, or homing beacons, and had to fly within narrow corridors when making flights across country throughout the United Kingdom. Their only option, on such non-operational flights, was to rely on their compass and map-reading, and 'Fly by Bradshaw', which meant following the railway lines. ('Bradshaw' was the name of the national train time-table which hosts made a habit of leaving beside the beds of guests who were overstaying their welcome.)

One of the problems was that all railway lines led to Crewe, which was an important railway junction, equipped with one of the biggest concentrations of barrage balloons in the country. During one period of particularly bad weather, when pilots could follow the railway lines but could not see sufficiently far ahead to see where they were heading, thirty British aircraft were brought down by the barrage balloons there in one month. So when the balloons went up in war-time, they frightened both friend and foe alike, as well as aircrew returning from operational missions in aircraft with damaged navigational systems.

To climb on the bandwagon In many countries, the USA in particular, it has long been the custom for a band of musicians to play on a wagon as it moves through the streets, often ahead of a procession, to advertise a meeting, or speech to be made by a politician intent on winning votes, or some other important person advocating some cause. Local leaders, and dignitaries, often chose to show their support by climbing on the wagon. Nowadays, when anyone starts anything new which looks like being successful, others who see profit in the idea, or plan, jump or 'climb on the bandwagon' to attempt to reap the advantages.

To bandy words is to argue with someone. The phrase is used mainly negatively in everyday conversation. One tells someone that one is not going to bandy words with them.

Bandy was originally a game of hockey, and also a form of tennis, in which the ball was bandied (or struck) from one side to the other, with opponents trying to score off each other.

To bank on it is another way of saying that you can put your trust in something, and may rest assured that whatever you are contemplating, or have done, is secure and can be counted upon — in much the same way as money put into banks is safe.

The phrase goes back to the time of the first bankers, or money-changers, of the medieval Italian cities, who conducted their transactions from benches in the streets and market-place. The word 'bank' comes from *banco*, which is the Italian for 'bench'.

The first commercial bank, the Banco di Rialto, was established in 1587 in Venice, and banks were started subsequently in other European cities. The Bank of England was founded in the city of London in 1694, and acquired its present site in Threadneedle Street in 1724.

Wouldn't touch with a barge-pole In the 17th century a pair of tongs was the instrument with which people would not touch those whom they disliked, or distrusted. Two centuries later Charles Dickens was still using tongs in the phrase.

'Barge-pole' is comparatively recent usage and is an appropriate choice, for, being longer than tongs, it would be possible to keep people or objects one wishes to avoid, or regards with loathing, at a greater distance.

Barring the way *see* To BALK someone

Keeping at bay Plants and trees have been associated with powers of protection against disaster and as remedies against ills and disease for thousands of years. The Greeks and Romans believed that the Bay Laurel provided protection against thunderbolts, as this tree was never struck by lightning, so they wore its leaves as a head-covering during thunderstorms. Centuries later, bay trees came to be placed on or near homes.

The leaves of the Bay Laurel, or 'Sweet Bay', were also said to counteract plagues, and the phrase 'keeping at bay' arose from their widespread use during the Great Plague of London in 1665. Neither this nor any other medicines or cures worked, and the plague was believed to have killed over 90,000 people.

Two hundred years passed before medical science discovered that the plague had been carried by fleas which came to this country in the fur of black rats arriving in ships from plague infested areas of the world. A bite from one of these fleas was almost certain to result in the death of the victim.

Fortunately, the black rats were killed by another rat, the common brown rat. When the garbage in the streets of London was cleaned up at the time of the Plague, this deprived the black rats of their main food source so that many died of starvation, and the brown rats set to work

[16]

attacking the survivors. The winter of 1665 was a cold one and after the Great Fire of London, the following year, the plague died away.

When London was rebuilt with wider and cleaner streets, and precautions were taken to prevent rats coming ashore (through the use of metal discs on the mooring ropes of ships in harbour) the plague was 'kept at bay'. The phrase continued in use until modern times.

On one's beam-ends is to be in a difficult or dangerous situation. The phrase comes from the days of the wooden sailing ships. The beams are the horizontal timbers, stretching across the ship, which supported the deck, and joined the sides. During gales and heavy seas, vessels were often thrown almost completely on to their side, to the point where they were on their beam-ends, with the beams in an upright position instead of lying horizontally, and the ship almost capsizing.

To have a bean feast In Shakespeare's time Christmas festivities lasted until the twelfth day — epiphany — during which time work ceased and everyone, of all ages and from every background, gave themselves over to feasting and merrymaking. Twelfth night itself was a very special occasion for merriment and feasting of various kinds. One of the customs was to make a special cake in which a bean and a pea were placed. As the cake was divided up, any man lucky enough to have the piece with the bean was crowned 'king', until midnight, and any woman receiving the pea was 'queen'. Hence the expression 'a bean feast' which, in time, also covered the annual dinner given by an employer to his workpeople. The expression 'full of beans' meant to be very lively and in high spirits.

Twelfth night cakes are still made in some counties. In London they are made in memory of Robert Baddeley, a cook who later became an actor, who left £100, when he died in 1794, to provide wine and cake on every twelfth night for the cast playing at the Drury Lane Theatre, and even to this day this has been continued.

The bean cake has also featured in the other ancient twelfth night custom, still carried on in several apple-growing districts, known as the 'wassailing of the apple trees', to ensure a plentiful crop of fruit. The countryfolk go to the orchards at dusk with shot-guns, metal trays, kettles and an ample supply of cider. After selecting one tree, to represent all, everyone assembled drinks its health and then throws cider over its roots. This is followed by the placing of a piece of the twelfth night bean cake in one of the forks in its branches.

After firing their guns through the topmost branches to drive away demons, as much noise as possible is made by beating the trays, pans and kettles, as well as by shouting, and a final singing of the wassail song. Everyone usually enjoys themselves so much that they go on to other trees to repeat the ceremony.

To beard someone (or the lion in his den) Although beard growth is determined by heredity, a luxuriant beard has long been looked upon as a sign of virility, physical strength and dignity. Apart from Peter the Great, Czar of Russia (1672–1725), who thought otherwise and imposed a tax on beards, it was considered outrageous in most countries to so much as touch a man's beard. 'To beard someone' and do so deliberately was the height of insult and an act of total defiance.

TO BEARD THE LION IN HIS DEN is an extension of the phrase, meaning to come face to face, and therefore in close proximity, with someone and oppose them openly by saying exactly what one feels, fearlessly and regardless of the consequences.

As beards have come back into fashion today, they can be used more positively, for, to 'swear by one's beard' was once an assurance of good faith.

An eager beaver is used, both in America and Britain, to describe anyone who is exceptionally keen and industrious, or who volunteers to undertake all manner of jobs, and then puts everything they have got into them. Beavers are among the most intelligent and hard working of animals as well as being remarkable 'engineers', able to build dams, houses, canals, and cut down trees. Besides rearing their own litter of three or four at a time, they also take over the raising of orphaned beavers.

Although the beaver is a relative of the squirrel, it is larger, up to 2 ft (·66 m) long. It is amphibious, with webbed hind feet for swimming, and a large flat tail used as a rudder, also to 'slap' the water as a warning signal to others when danger is present.

One of the outstanding skills the beaver possesses is in cutting down trees and building dams. Standing on their hind legs, they are able to reach up and gnaw round and round the trunk of a tree with their sharp incisor teeth until the tree, often as much as 18 inches (46 cm) in diameter, is ready to fall. Then they set to work lopping off the branches and cutting the trunk into conveniently sized lengths which they can drag into the water to build a dam. They do this by anchoring the trunks across the stream and then building up alternate layers of mud, stones, and timber until the dam is high enough. The dam not only serves to ensure sufficient water in which to transport the logs, but also as a protection to secure the house (known as their 'lodge') and food store from predators. The lodge is made in the same way as the dam, with wood, mud and stones, and has two underwater passages and doorways leading to a conveniently sized main accommodation room and second area which serves as the food store or larder.

The word 'eager' is derived through the French *aigre* from the Latin *acer*, meaning sharp, keen.

To get out of bed on the wrong side This figure of speech refers to anyone who is moody or bad-tempered for the day, and for whom everything seems to go wrong for no apparent reason. It is based on the old superstition that it is unlucky to get out on the left side, or to touch the floor with the left foot first — this was because the left hand side was associated with the west, where the sun sets, symbolizing death.

Many people are still superstitious about the placing of a bed. To position it pointing east and west would seem to be the answer, then neither side would be the wrong side to get out of, but there are many who believe that this alignment causes trouble; other people consider that a bed pointing north and south makes for a restless night, accompanied by nightmares.

It's Bedlam is used to describe any chaotic scene, or state of affairs, which results in disorder and ends in a turmoil. Its origin is anything but pleasant and is associated with the Hospital of St Mary of Bethlehem, London, which was founded in 1247 as a priory and converted 300 years later into a lunatic asylum. When extra revenue was needed for its upkeep, a tragic error was made in deciding to raise the money by charging members of the public two pence each admission as sightseers. Although £400 was obtained in this way, from thousands of visitors each year, the sightseers were not taken on conducted tours but allowed, instead, to wander at will. The result was that many ridiculed the patients.

The word 'patients' was also unfortunate, for 'Bedlam', as the hospital was known, was a place of detention, without any treatment available to the inmates. The keepers were worse than the sightseers and made a habit of beating, chaining, and starving them. The proper care and humane treatment of people suffering from mental illness did not come into being in hospitals and institutions until late in the 19th century and, even to this day, there is still a lot that has yet to be understood by both the public at large and the medical profession.

A bee in one's bonnet — A busy bee — Queen bee — The bee's knees — To make a beeline As the honey-bee has always been important to man, it is not surprising that it should be the subject of many everyday phrases and expressions. The effect of having a stinging bee trapped under one's bonnet, or hat, can well be imagined. To have A BEE IN ONE'S BONNET is to be crazed or obsessed with some idea or subject which fully occupies the mind so that one cannot stop thinking or talking about it. Of course, these ideas may seem quite irrational to others.

Honey-bees are incredible insects. Those in the colony of a domestic hive work hard for the benefit of the entire colony, numbering around 60,000. The hive itself, with its honeycomb structure, is a masterpiece of architecture. The work in building, maintaining and using it, gathering nectar, pollinating flowers, and making honey and wax calls for the maximum effort in the shortest possible time. Hence the expression 'as busy as a bee' and A BUSY BEE describes an extremely active person.

Worker bees (sterile females) soon wear themselves out with this hard work and only live for four or five weeks if hatched in the summer, or six months if hatched in the autumn and they survive the winter. The queen who works as hard, and longer, than her subjects may live for five years, and life in the hive centres around her.

On Royal Air Force Stations the chief WAAF (now the WRAF) is called the QUEEN BEE by all male and female personnel — the phrase originating during World War II.

Although the real queen bee is surrounded by males, she chooses to ignore them in the hive. When she soars high in the air on her wedding flight, the drones and those from neighbouring hives follow her, but only the fittest are able to reach the height she can. For centuries it was believed that only a single mating took place, but nowadays it is known that up to as many as ten drones will mate with the queen on this flight. Once this is over, she returns to the hive and sets about laying up to 2,000 eggs a day. The drones die immediately after mating, which is their sole function in the colony.

The origin of the phrase THE BEE'S KNEES is obscure but probably connected with the fact they have pollen containers on their legs. For, when they seek the nectar in flowers, pollen rubs off on their bodies. To remove it, they clean it off with their legs for storage in special pollen baskets, which are located on the outside surface of their rear legs, ready to be carried back to the hive. The process of removal involves much bending of the knees and is carried out with great precision — it is possible that the expression came about as a result of this. 'The bee's knees' is not generally a description of one person by another, but is used to describe someone who considers themself to be 'the bee's knees' because they are so clever.

Anyone who MAKES A BEELINE for something is acting like a bee in going in a straight line towards something (the hive), or whatever they are intent on reaching. The bees are the real 'bee's knees' because their expertise in navigation, when going from one point to another, makes use of the sun and the pattern of light in the sky, and built-in corrections allowing for the movement of the sun enable them to keep heading in the right direction.

According to Mrs Beeton This phrase, which has been in regular use since the 1860s, is associated with an outstanding publishing success story — and a remarkable young woman. Isabella Mary Mayson was born in London in 1836, and subsequently educated at Heidelberg where she studied under Sir Julius Benedict and became an accomplished pianist. That in itself was no mean achievement and, indirectly, it was to stand her in good stead. However, we do not remember this lady for her music, but for the major contribution she was to make to our homes, their running and, above all, to the enjoyment of our food.

When she was twenty she married a publisher, Samuel Orchart Beeton. After writing a number of articles for a magazine he had founded, she spent four years writing her *Book of Household Management* which, apart from including valuable tips on domestic economy, concentrated on cookery. The book contained over 4,000 recipes and immediately received acclaim everywhere, becoming established as the most famous of all English cookery books. Earlier editions included recipes for soup for the poor at a cost of about $1\frac{1}{2}$ pennies a gallon, so the claim that all her recipes are extravagant is not quite correct.

Cookery has often been likened to music. Just as a composer selects and blends the notes to produce a pleasing harmony so, too, a good cook draws on ingredients, either in a dominant or supportive role, to blend, compliment, and flavour to achieve a harmonious and perfect recipe. 'According to Mrs Beeton . . .' was a phrase used by experienced cooks and novices alike to preface a counsel of perfection.

Mrs Beeton was twenty-five years old when her book was first published in volume form, in 1861. Since then it has run into many editions and, though she saw something of its success, she died, when only twenty-nine years' old, of puerperal fever, a week after the birth of her fourth son.

Her book became a classic; a revised and greatly enlarged centenary edition, published in 1960, still influences cooks today.

Bell, book, and candle During ceremonial excommunications from the Roman Catholic Church, the bell was tolled, the book closed, and the candle extinguished by throwing it to the ground.

When the phrase is used in everyday speech, it usually accompanies a severe reprimand, involving total exclusion or rejection, in which the person making the exhortation is severely laying down, or upholding, the law and having the last word.

Bell the cat When Archibald Douglas, fifth Earl of Angus said 'I shall bell the cat,' at a meeting of Scottish nobles, in 1482, he could have been more cautious and said 'I'll see which way the cat jumps' — but not so. Instead, he indicated that he was prepared to take a risk and face danger himself, for the common good.

The phrase arose from the fable in which some mice got together and suggested that a bell should be put round a cat's neck so that they would have prior warning of danger when it approached. Although all the mice agreed that it was a good idea, none had the courage to do it himself though it would be for the benefit of them all.

As clear as a bell means that one understands perfectly the explanation which has just been given, even though it may have been on the most complicated of subjects. The phrase is derived from the clear tone and carrying power of church bells. It is also used sometimes to describe perfect visibility on a bright, clear, day, although 'as clear as crystal' might be more appropriate.

The opposite would be to say 'it's as clear as mud', meaning that the explanation is so confused that one cannot understand it, or that one literally cannot see because visibility is obscured by mist or fog.

To hang on the bell means to hang on at all costs, in a desperate situation, no matter how bleak the outlook, or impossible the odds.

The expression arose from an incident during the Wars of the Roses (1455–1485) in which the signal for the execution of a prisoner of noble birth, who had been captured in battle, was to be announced by the tolling of the curfew bell in the local church. When a reprieve was sought at the last moment, the messenger who had been despatched to obtain a pardon from the king still had some way to go on horseback. Miraculously, the bell did not ring that night and the messenger reached his destination, and returned with a reprieve.

Later, it was discovered that the condemned man's life had been saved by his sweetheart who had 'hung on to the bell' in the belfry to stop it ringing.

That rings a bell This expression is used when some happening which seems familiar is recalled to mind, even though it may have occurred many years ago. The phrase can also be said of an object that has been forgotten and then when rediscovered, it brings back a memory.

Bells have served as reminders for centuries. Besides summoning people to church, they have been used to signal that fires must be put out at a fixed hour in the evening before going to bed, and as an alarm to signal the news of military attack. In times of martial law, there were curfew bells to remind civilians of the hour when they must remain indoors. They were also rung during happier times on festive occasions, and were harbingers of good news.

Saved by the bell means to be saved from a difficult situation at the last possible moment.

One of the strangest examples of this occurred in England in the late 17th century, during the reign of William and Mary, when a sentry on duty at Windsor Castle was accused of being asleep on duty. His defence at his courts-martial was that as he had heard the clock of St Paul's, in London, strike *thirteen* at midnight, he could not have been asleep.

Although town, city, and country life was comparatively quiet in those days, allowing sound to travel over a considerable distance, the court ridiculed the idea that the bells of St Pauls could carry over the twenty miles between London and Windsor, and sentenced him to death.

While imprisoned and awaiting execution, some citizens of London heard of the sentry's story and his denial of the charge; they verified, to the satisfaction of the authorities, that the clock of St Paul's did, in fact, strike *thirteen* instead of twelve on that particular night. The sentry was 'saved by the bell', released, and lived to the ripe old age of 102.

Today, the expression is associated, by most people, with the ringing of the bell at the end of each round in a boxing match.

To go berserk is to work oneself up into a frenzy over something. Originally, it referred to Viking warriors who worked themselves into a fighting fever and went into battle recklessly, without armour, to show their contempt for the foe, clad only in a 'berserkr', or bear-sark, which was a bearskin coat.

Bites *see* To make two bites of a CHERRY

[23]

To be blackballed When someone is 'blackballed' it means that their application for membership of a club, or similar organization, has been rejected. The expression comes from the early practice of voting with coloured balls. (The word 'ballot' means 'little ball'). When members were considering a new applicant, they placed a ball of their choice in an urn which served as a ballot box. A white ball denoted a favourable vote, and black ball an adverse vote. The rules were strict; even if only one ball in the urn was found to be black, when the votes were counted, the applicant was rejected.

Until 1872, voters in parliamentary and local elections went to the polling station and announced publicly the name of the candidate for whom they voted. This gave rise to vote buying, and reprisals in many instances from landlords, employers, or other people of influence, if a voter dared to select anyone other than their candidate. In 1872, voting papers and the ballot box were introduced as we know them today, which ensured secrecy, to put an end to this intimidating system.

To blaze a trail Explorers travelling through unknown country used to mark trees along their route by chipping bark off them, so that others following would know which way to go. The white wood revealed was known as a 'blaze'. Today, anyone who pioneers anything is known as a 'trail blazer'.

Bless you! It has long been the custom when anyone sneezes to say 'bless you', although we do not accompany it with the removal of our hats and a bow, as was the practice of the gentlemen in 17th-century England.

Sometimes we cannot help sneezing not only once, but several times in succession. Some unfortunate chronic sneezers continue do so for days on end, or even for many months. Sneezing has been regarded since ancient times as a signal from the gods which foretold good or bad luck, depending on the circumstances, time, and number of sneezes. The ancient Greeks and Romans were tolerant of sneezers and made a point of wishing the sufferer good health and fortune.

> Speak roughly to your little boy,
> And beat him when he sneezes;
> He only does it to annoy,
> Because he knows it teases.

The advice of the duchess in Lewis Carroll's *Alice in Wonderland* does seem harsh, on the other hand, most people would agree that sneezing is a most objectionable habit. They would consider it even more so if they

[24]

knew that it has been estimated that particles shot from the nose travel at a speed of just over 100 mph (161 km/h). The duchess in the story *does* beat her little boy when he sneezes but she excuses herself by pointing out that 'he can thoroughly enjoy the pepper when he pleases!'

By the early 19th century another expression had come into being, 'not to be sneezed at', meaning something was not to be disregarded, or treated with contempt, as it might well come up to standard. As people tend to turn up their noses or crinkle them when sneezing, or when in doubt, this could provide a likely explanation for the origin of the expression.

A stumbling block *see* to BALK someone

To blow one's top — Let off steam Like volcanoes, which can lie dormant for long periods, man tends to 'erupt' now and again. When he does so he loses control of his temper, and BLOWS HIS TOP. This anger may be caused by others, or something he has done, or failed to do. The milder form is less devastating; when annoyed he might just LET OFF STEAM by throwing something.

Volcanoes, of course, may literally 'blow their top', or 'let off steam'. When they are about to erupt there is a deafening explosion followed by the plug (or crust of lava) being blown out of the crater as a result of the enormous pressure which has been built up inside by both steam and gas.

There are more than 500 known active volcanoes throughout the world, including 80 that are submarine. Some have remained dormant for centuries before erupting again. Amongst the most famous volcanic eruptions were those at Santorini, in 1470 BC, and Krakatoa in AD 1883. (*See* once in a blue moon). The eruption of Vesuvius in AD 79, which buried Pompeii and Herculaneum under pumice and ash, is probably the best known. These two Roman cities were uncovered by archaeologists almost seventeen centuries later, and we can still see their remains today.

Blue-blooded Anyone who has 'blue blood' is deemed to be of noble or royal descent. The phrase originally referred to people of pure Spanish ancestry who had no Moorish admixture. It is based on the fact that people who have a light skin appear to have blue blood in their veins.

Blue-stocking When anyone was referred to as a 'blue-stocking' the term was used disparagingly to describe a woman of learning, high intellect, and literary tastes. A society of that name, which adopted blue stockings as its badge, was founded in Venice during the 15th century; the idea and the badge were adopted by women in Paris towards the end of the following century. England was slow to follow until the middle of the 18th century, when erudite women met in private houses to discuss and further their interests rather than pass the time (or, in their view, waste it) playing cards or sewing.

The original stockings, used as clothing, were shapeless tubes of cloth or other materials sewn together. Henry II (1154–1189) was the first English king to wear a pair of knit silk stockings. Nothing was heard of stockings again until the reign of Henry VIII (1509–1547). Sir Thomas Gresham presented Edward VI (1547–1553) with a pair, and they were much thought of.

The development of stockings was furthered by the Rev. William Lee, of Nottinghamshire who felt that he could improve on the time taken by women to hand-knit stockings with their two or three needles. He invented a machine to do the work using eight needles and was so pleased with the result that he presented Queen Elizabeth with a pair. She, however, had been furnished by her silk woman with a pair of *silk* stockings in the third year of her reign, which she had described 'as marvellous delicate wear', while those from the curate were of coarse worsted.

Lee made another machine, with more needles, to knit stockings finer and faster, and then presented the queen with a pair of silk stockings. Although pleased with the result, she did not feel disposed to grant the inventor a patent or any assistance. The conventional stocking hand-knitters feared that it would spoil their trade and drove him away. He was forced to take his machine to France and is said to have died of grief. Lee's invention did not die with him for its use spread subsequently in England and gave birth to the mechanisation of the British hosiery industry.

Men continued to wear silk stockings after Queen Elizabeth's reign. James VI of Scotland (before he became James I) liked them so well that it was said of him that he danced them into holes. He also boosted their popularity by borrowing a pair from the Earl of Mar in order to receive the English ambassador dressed in them, declaring 'For ye would not, sure, that your king should appear as a scrub before strangers.'

The fashion of wearing black silk stockings in England is said to have been introduced by Henrietta Maria of France, queen of Charles I (1625–1649). Indeed Charles I and his son Charles II (1660–1685) seldom wore any other type of stocking.

When American soldiers, sailors and airmen brought the first nylons over during World War II, English girls went wild with delight and couldn't have prized them more highly. When the war ended, nylons remained in short supply for some years before the British hosiery industry were able to manufacture them in sufficient quantities to meet the demand. Although the original shades were flesh coloured, blue nylons immediately became popular when they were introduced, though the original 'blue-stocking' image no longer referred disparagingly to women of learning and high literary tastes, but, flatteringly, to those of high fashion.

A bolt from the blue refers to something which comes as complete surprise, or arrives unexpectedly. The origin of the phrase is likely to have arisen from the phenomena of 'shooting stars', lightning and meteorites, which provide such spectacular displays in the sky and arrive without warning on earth.

About 150 meteorites, which penetrate the earth's atmosphere without burning up, fall on the land surface of the earth each year. Most are small, but the largest known meteorite, measuring 9 ft (2.74 m) by 8 ft (2.43 m) and weighing in the region of 59 tons (60 tonnes), was found in south-west Africa in 1920.

Even small 'bolts from the blue' can provide an astonishing display — one of iron, no larger than the size of the head of a pin, can shine with a light as brilliant as that of a star of the first order.

A rare form of lightning, which resembles a ball of fire and sometimes appears on the masts and yards of ships, was interpreted by sailors as a visitation from heaven and named after their parton saint, St Elmo, who died at sea during a severe storm. During his last moments, St Elmo promised the crew that he would reveal himself to them in some way after he died, if destiny dictated that they would survive the storm. Shortly after his death, a bright light glowed around the mast and this strange phenomenon is still known by sailors today as 'St Elmo's Fire'.

Although modern scientific knowledge tells us that it is caused by electrical discharges during storms, we know little of the phenomenon called 'ball lightning' which, as its name implies, looks just like a ball of fire, but glows and moves slowly, often horizontally, just above the ground — even inside houses and across rooms. The explanation of this 'bolt from the blue' which comes as a complete surprise, and arrives unexpectedly, is still an unsolved problem. Ball lightning has even been filmed moving slowly inside the room of a house, and the film was shown on television, but it remains a mystery.

[27]

To make no bones about — A bone to pick with someone — A bone of contention The expression TO MAKE NO BONES ABOUT, which originated over 450 years ago, means to get straight to the point without hesitation or restraint. In its less agressive form it can also be used to imply that one is ready to accept a suggestion, proposal, or point of view without raising an objection, or putting any obstacles in the way. The lack of hindrance in both cases is said to have been likened to a bowl of soup in which the bones have been removed, thus enabling the contents to be swallowed immediately, and without difficulty.

A BONE TO PICK WITH SOMEONE indicates matters of dispute, and usually results in a heated argument at best, or even a fight, as when two dogs confront each other over a single bone. It is as well to remember the old saying that 'when two dogs fight for a bone, a third often runs away with it'. So one needs to be on one's guard in more ways than one. By the early 18th century, any dispute which remained unsettled became known as A BONE OF CONTENTION.

To boot When these two words are added on to the end of a sentence, they mean 'in addition' or 'what's more', to stress the point being made. For example, 'The seafood dishes available (at such and such a restaurant) not only provide wide variety; they are the best in the country to boot'. The old English word *bot* means advantage, or to the good.

The boot is on the other leg This phrase, of 19th century origin, is used to denote that the situation has changed — that the position is, in fact, precisely the opposite of what it seemed.

The original boots or shoes produced in England were made to fit either foot, without thought for comfort, and remained that way until towards the end of the 18th century when 'right' and 'left' lasts were introduced. It seems likely that the expression came into being as a result of this.

To hang up one's boots denotes retirement, usually of people who have pursued outdoor occupations, such as footballers and jockeys. As sportsmen have to hang up their boots, or 'retire' earlier than most people in other jobs and professions, it does not necessarily mean that they are going to give up work altogether. A jockey, for instance, might give up riding in races, but become a trainer. Others, no longer taking an active part in a particular sport, might hang up their boots and embark

[28]

on another career, such as becoming a writer, journalist or commentator, thus making use of their specialist knowledge.

Born *see* Born with a silver SPOON in one's mouth

Bottoms up *see* Eat, drink, and be MERRY

To be bowler-hatted — A golden handshake — To be drummed out As the bowler hat, known in the USA as the 'Derby' hat, is associated with Civvie Street (civilian life), TO BE BOWLER-HATTED is to be demobilized, or discharged from the armed forces with a gratuity before one's commission has reached its normal termination. The civilian equivalent is A GOLDEN HANDSHAKE in which an executive is given a handsome payment when asked to leave a company or organization before their time.

TO BE DRUMMED OUT, on the other hand, applied to anyone who was cashiered, or dismissed in disgrace from the regiment, to the solemn accompaniment of the beat of drums.

To get down to brass tacks — Not worth a brass farthing To get down to the essential details and real business of anything, or come straight to the point when discussing some project or other is TO GET DOWN TO BRASS TACKS. It has nothing to do with 'hitting nails on the head' and, in fact, originated in the old-fashioned drapers' shops. Once the customer had made up their mind about which cloth to purchase, the shop assistant got down to brass tacks by measuring the amount of cloth required against brass-headed nails which were evenly spaced along the counter.

In time, the brass tacks were replaced by a brass rule built into the edge of the counter, and many shops and stores still use them today. They were scaled in measurements up to 3 ft (36 in) long, representing a yard. The term 'yardstick' came into the English language as a basis for actual measurement as well as a term meaning a basis on which to make comparisons.

Brass has also been used as a slang term for money since the end of the 17th century, when England's coinage was debased by the issue of brass pennies, halfpennies, and farthings. As the latter was worth virtually nothing it led to the introduction of the phrase NOT WORTH A BRASS FARTHING.

Many phrases are connected with brass, such as the North Country English one of 'where there's muck there's brass', meaning that it is possible to make money out of anything if one works hard enough and is not afraid to dirty one's hands.

[29]

Bricks *see* Making bricks without STRAW

Bristol fashion *see* ALL SHIP SHAPE and Bristol fashion

The buck stops here Harry S. Truman, President of the USA (1945–1953), originated many phrases, including 'the buck stops here' which also became popular in Britain. (*See also* 'If you can't stand the heat, keep out of the kitchen.) The person on whose desk the buck rests must be prepared to take responsibility and not 'pass the buck' on to someone else.

The original 'buck' was a buckhorn knife passed around the table in certain card games. It was placed in front of the player whose turn it was to deal the cards and see that the stakes for all the players were placed in the pool.

To kick the bucket The bucket in this phrase does not refer to the vessel used for carrying water, but to the bucket beam, or wooden frame, on which pigs were hung after slaughter. Anyone who has 'kicked the bucket', therefore, has died. 'To snuff it' also means to die, but is an easier expression to understand as it refers to the snuffing out of a candle.

Bumpers all round, and no heel taps *see* Eat, drink, and be MERRY

Gone for a Burton This phrase originated in the RAF during World War II and was used extensively to ease the tension in squadrons whenever a pilot or aircrew member was killed, or went missing. Burton-on-Trent, in Staffordshire, is famous for its beer and the expression 'He's gone for a Burton' meant that anyone who had failed to return to base, without news, after carrying out a mission had gone for a drink, or 'bought it' and been killed.

The 'drink' also referred to the sea, and anyone shot down over the water without having been seen to escape by parachute was said to have 'gone for a Burton', or 'gone into the drink'.

Bury *see* To bury the HATCHET

Bury *see* To bury one's HEAD in the sand

Bush *see* A good WINE needs no bush

A busman's holiday is to spend one's free time, or holiday, doing precisely the same thing as one does at work.

Everyone loves a horse, and during the day of the old horse-drawn buses some of the drivers became so attached to their horses that they made a point of seeing that they were being treated properly by going along as a passenger on their own bus, on their days off.

A piece of cake is equivalent to the phrase 'money for old rope' and refers to a job which requires little effort for a profitable reward. Something which represents easy money or 'money for jam' for doing something which is as easy as eating a piece of cake.

A 'cakewalk' or 'to take the cake', means to beat everything, and refers to the custom of Negro couples of the southern states of the USA walking gracefully round a cake. The judges awarded the prize of the cake to the best-dressed couple who did the cakewalk in the most elegant manner.

Don't call us, we'll call you — The cheque's in the post — It's in the pipeline — It's going through the computer DON'T CALL US, WE'LL CALL YOU originated in the heyday of the Hollywood film industry, when young hopefuls set out to seek their fame and fortune there. It subsequently came to be used through the whole theatrical world. It was used as a polite way of saying thank you to applicants who had come for an audition but who were not up to standard or considered suitable. The phrase meant, in effect, the precise opposite of what it implied as the speaker had no intention of telephoning the applicant, or getting in touch at all. It is similarly used in the business world to cut short an interview, or at its close, when an applicant has failed to impress or come up to the standard required for the job being applied for.

Another 'reverse-meaning' phrase is THE CHEQUE'S IN THE POST. If it is still 'in the post' some days or weeks later and the person expecting it telephones to find out what is happening, they may be told that IT'S IN

THE PIPELINE (in the process of delivery, like the flow of oil through pipelines from the wells to the tankers, the refinery, and eventually the consumer). If this fails to reassure, the alternative excuse often used is that IT'S GOING THROUGH THE COMPUTER. As computers were invented to speed things up the excuse can only be interpreted as a delaying tactic. There is little the person awaiting the cheque can do except be patient and hope that it will eventually arrive before much further delay.

To carry the can is to receive the blame for a misdeed or mistake for which others are responsible. The phrase, which is still used widely in everyday life, was originally a military one, and referred to the person chosen to carry the beer cans to and fro for replenishing when they were empty. (A 'can' was a nickname for a simpleton, during World War I.) Those landed with such menial tasks were usually rookies (raw recruits) with insufficient experience to stand up for themselves, and they had no alternative but to do as they were told, so they were left to carry the can for others.

Not fit to hold the candle Before electricity became widely available, one person frequently held a candle to assist another when carrying out work. An apprentice would do this for his master craftsman, for instance. There were always some apprentices who would never make the grade, no matter how long their apprenticeship; they were, therefore, not fit to hold the candle for their masters. The phrase is still used to describe one person who can only be compared with another unfavourably.

The game is not worth the candle dates from the 17th century, when gambling games were lit by candles. Any player who was losing had reason to consider that the game was not worth the cost of the candle. The phrase is used more generally today to apply to any enterprise or venture which is not worth the cost or effort involved as the results are likely to be poor.

To paddle your own canoe is advice to get on with something through your own efforts and not rely on others. It was first used by the English naval captain and novelist Frederick Marryat (1792–1848), when he wrote 'Every man paddle his own canoe' in his story *Settlers in Canada*.

When a female polar bear scents danger she jumps into the water and her cub holds her tail while she tows it to safety. If there is no danger she expects the cub to 'paddle its own canoe'. If it is too lazy, or refuses to swim by itself, she ducks its head under the water and prods it.

[32]

To win in a canter is an expression used in horse-racing, in which the first horse past the post wins easily — in a canter. The word 'canter' came into being from the easy gallop (or Canterbury pace) at which pilgrims rode to the shrine of St Thomas à Becket at Canterbury Cathedral.

When Chaucer wrote his *Canterbury Tales* about a company of pilgrims making this journey, the party assembled at the Tabard Inn at Southwark in London and each agreed to tell two tales on the outward journey and two returning. The prize of a free supper on the homeward journey was offered to the pilgrim who told the best story. Although Chaucer started to write this work in 1373, and continued to do so for the next twenty years, it was never completed, beyond twenty-two narratives, interspersed with conversation pieces, and we have none of the tales told on the homeward journey.

The expression 'to win in a canter' is also used today, to describe anyone who romps home and wins hands down, or achieves their goal easily.

To set one's cap at — To cap it all During the 18th century, it was observed that 'a woman who endeavours to attract the notice of any particular man, is said to set her cap at him'. In the following century William Thackeray used the phrase in *Vanity Fair*: 'That girl is setting her cap at you'. In those times women always wore head-coverings on social occasions, and those who wished to attract a suitor made a point of wearing the most attractive caps they could obtain in order to become the focus of attention. Women still set their caps at men during the 1920s and 1930s and the phrase remained in frequent use.

As the cap is worn on the head it is symbolic of the 'top' or summit of excellence. 'To cap' anything is, therefore, to go one better, while TO CAP IT ALL can either mean to surpass all that has been said or done before, or (in its sarcastic and opposite sense) to ruin everything by trying to be too ambitious or clever.

Cap *see* A FEATHER in your cap

Captain *see* captain of one's SOUL

Cart *see* To put the cart before the HORSE

On the carpet Anyone who finds himself 'on the carpet' will wish, no doubt, that they had behaved themselves, rather than face the severe reprimand from their superior for their misdeeds. Originally, the carpet was the one in the reception room of the master or mistress of the house, who would summon a servant there to be scolded.

In Victorian times, and even during the earlier part of the present century, the exclamation of astonishment and disapproval, 'hoity-toity', was often introduced into the scolding for unruly conduct or insubordination (from the old English *hoit*, meaning to be riotous).

Carpet-baggers This name was given in the USA to the politicians and financial adventurers from the north who sought office or profit in the southern states after the Civil War ended in 1865. The phrase originally referred to unwelcome strangers who came to exploit a region and its inhabitants, when they had no rights or qualifications to settle in the area. Many had nothing more than their travelling bag, made of carpet, which contained their belongings.

In subsequent years, a candidate for Parliament in Britain who was a complete stranger to the constituency came to be called a carpet-bagger by their opponents. Today, however, it is not uncommon for a candidate to seek, and win, election in a constituency without having lived there or without having any former links with the area.

The phrase seldom refers to politicians today. It is used more generally to describe anyone trying to get into a position of authority to obtain personal advantage when they have nothing to contribute, and no special qualifications, and may act against the wishes of the majority of the people concerned.

Cat *see* BELL the cat

A cat has nine lives The ancient Egyptians tamed cats, more than 3,000 years ago, and treated them as members of their families. When a pet cat died they embalmed it before burial and the family went into mourning. To kill a cat was a crime punishable by death. With such care and protection bestowed on them, cats were unlikely to die prematurely, and their natural instincts for survival in situations where most other animals would perish brought about the belief that they had nine lives.

Besides being cautious and wily, cats are extremely agile, with a quick turn of speed when necessary. Even when they fall, or have to leap from a considerable height, they manage to survive. High-speed photography has shown that when a cat falls, even in an upsidedown position, it somehow manages to turn in the air and land on its feet which are padded to cushion the impact. Sometimes they use their tail, outstretched before their feet, to lessen the shock.

When they make mistakes they still seem to survive. One cat being chased by a dog was observed to dash out of a front garden into the road, becoming entangled in the rear back-wheel of a passing car, in the days when the spokes were fewer, wider, and spaced further apart. After whirling round for several revolutions and travelling some way it managed to extricate itself, land on its feet, and bound off, 'like a cat on hot bricks', over the wall of another garden on the opposite side of the road, completely unharmed. Cats don't always survive dangers, of course, but they do so more often than not, hence their 'nine lives'.

Grin like a Cheshire cat The phrase was popular long before Lewis Carroll's Alice encountered the cat in Wonderland, which vanished slowly until all she could see was its grin.

Many stories have been woven around the noble cat, the furry companion which records indicate were first tamed by the Egyptians thirteen centuries before Christ.

'Cheshire' comes into the saying because the English county's cheeses were once marked with the head of a cat. But the true meaning of the saying has nothing to do with the story of Alice, or with a cheese as the 'cat' was a man and the original saying was 'grin like a Cheshire Caterling'. This was the name of one of Richard III's forest rangers, 500 years ago, who was a skilled swordsman and not only a terrifying individual for poachers and others to come across, but also a man with a huge, hideous grin. During subsequent years caterling became shortened to 'cat' and continued to be used in everyday speech.

Not enough room to swing a cat is a phrase still used to describe the confined space of any room, in a private or public building, which is too small to live or work in even if minimum standards of comfort are acceptable. The cat has nothing to do with the animal but refers to the whip used on board ships of the British Navy for administering punishment. The whip began as a cat-of-three-tails but, by the end of the 17th century, had become a cat-of-nine-tails. This harsh form of punishment was continued until 1875.

Catch 22 Anyone who finds themself in a situation which can be described as 'Catch 22' is faced with a choice between equally unattractive alternatives; either one will leave them in a difficulty, or in a very unpleasant situation, and no other choice is possible. The phrase was brought to life in the title of a novel written by Joseph Heller, in which the American pilots at an airbase towards the end of World War II were under acute strain through being forced to fly an excessive number of missions, beyond endurance. The catch, or dilemma, lay in the fact that there was no way to avoid these missions except to be diagnosed as insane, or to be killed in air combat. Any pilot who appeared to be mad could stop fighting and be sent home. On the other hand, if a pilot refused to fly and asked to go home (so that he would not be killed) this proved to the authorities that he was not mad, and he would be forced by his superiors to continue fighting.

Odysseus (known later by the Romans as Ulysses) was faced with a similar dilemma. While he was king of a small island off the west coast of Greece, he was summoned by his brother chieftans to join in the war against the Trojans. Unwilling to leave his young wife, and little son Telemachus, to fight in a foreign land, he feigned insanity. When a prince named Palamedes came for him, he discovered Odysseus ploughing the sand on the seashore, which he had sown with salt, with an ox and an ass yoked together. When Palamedes took the baby Telemachus and laid him in the direct line of the next furrow to be ploughed, Odysseus quickly turned the plough aside which proved that he was not really insane.

Odysseus was one of the greatest Greek warriors; it was he who conceived the idea of the 'wooden horse', and was amongst those who hid within it, making it possible to capture the city of Troy.

Tennyson's poem *Ulysses* reflects on the thoughts of the Greek hero in old age, as he looks back into the past, and forward into the future, when it is 'not too late to seek a newer world' . . . 'To strive, to seek, to find, and not to yield'.

By a long chalk If anyone wins, or accomplishes, something 'by a long chalk', it means that they have won easily, or completed something thoroughly. The reference to chalk comes from its use to chalk up points scored in a game. Chalk marks were also used to indicate the stages in the progress in some job or undertaking, before the introduction of pencils. When the phrase is used in its negative sense of 'not by a long chalk', it indicates that the job still requires many more chalk marks and, thus, has a long way to go.

Chance *see* To chance one's ARM

Don't change horses in mid-stream To try and change horses in this situation is obviously difficult and unwise, and the phrase advising against it suggests that one should think twice before changing one's opinion once things are under way. If one must make a change one should choose the right moment.

The phrase became famous when Abraham Lincoln told his critics, who were demanding a change in the presidency, that although many of his fellow Republicans were dissatisfied with his conduct of the American Civil War, they had renominated him and that the best thing was for him to remain as president rather than for them to elect to change horses in mid-stream.

To ring the changes is to change the order, or way of doing things, and thus provide variety, particularly when the same thing has to be repeated and different ways tried out, either to avoid monotony or, alternatively, to solve a problem.

The phrase comes from the art of bell-ringing and the practice of 'change ringing', which was established in England in the mid-17th century. As the number of bells in churches and cathedrals increased from three to five, then upwards to twelve, the number of changes that could be rung became enormous. Their totals can be reckoned quite simply, e.g. two bells provide two changes. As each bell is added, the number of changes possible is obtained by multiplying the total number of bells by the previous number of changes possible. Three bells, for example, requires three to be multiplied by the previous two, giving six changes: four bells $(4 \times 6) = 24$ changes . . . Five bells $(5 \times 24) = 120$ changes . . . Six bells $(6 \times 120) = 720$ changes.

Any tower containing 12 bells, such as the Bell Harry tower at Canterbury Cathedral, increases the number of changes possible to 479,001,600 — but it has been calculated that it would take thirty-eight years to ring all the changes.

To make two bites of a cherry In polite society, some 300 years ago, gentlemen who normally showed no restraint in devouring large quantities of food at meals, became hypocrites on formal occasions by making 'two bites of one cherry' when, in private, they would push a large quantity into their mouths at once.

To make two bites at so small an object as a cherry is obviously ridiculous, and the phrase warns against dividing anything that is too small to be worth dividing; or breaking off after one short spell of work on a job that is so easy it should be completed and disposed of in one go.

[37]

To have a chip on one's shoulder — A chip of the old block The first expression describes anyone who is disgruntled, resentful, bears a grudge, or has a grievance. The expression comes from the 19th century custom in America in which a boy wanting to give vent to his feelings used to place a chip on his shoulder, and fight any boy who dared to knock the wood off.

The other expression 'A CHIP OF THE OLD BLOCK' is used to describe a son resembling his father, or inheriting his talents. It was made famous when Edmund Burke (1729–1797), the great statesman, orator and writer, exclaimed excitedly, after listening to the first speech in the British Parliament of William Pitt the Younger, in 1781, that 'he was not merely a chip of the old block, but the old block itself'. The speech was made on 26 February 1781, when William Pitt was only twenty-one years old. He had become a Member of Parliament at twenty. He was to become Chancellor of the Exchequer at twenty-three, and Prime Minister when only twenty-four, the youngest man who has ever held that great office.

Praise from such a highly talented and respected man as Edmund Burke was praise indeed, for it is known that his writings influenced many great statesmen, including Sir Winston Churchill.

Chocks away originated in the early days of aviation and was used by service and civilian pilots alike and then, later, by the public in general, as the world became more and more air-minded. 'Chocks away' means that one wants to get going without delay, or get on with the job.

Chocks were blocks of wood, placed in front of the wheels of aeroplanes to stop forward movement when the engine was run up to test it before flight. When the pilot was ready, and had throttled back, he shouted the words, or waved his arms above his head, and the mechanics pulled on the ropes of each chock to remove them. The early aeroplanes had no brakes, so chocks were essential, but they continued to be used when brakes were fitted to single and multi-engined aircraft, both as a precaution to prevent the aircraft moving forward, as well as to save unnecessary wear on the brakes themselves.

During World War II when Hurricane, Spitfire, American and other fighters were run up against chocks, the pilot in the cockpit kept the tail from lifting off the ground by holding the control stick back as he opened the throttle. With so much power being unleashed, however, it was still necessary for one or two members of the ground crew to throw themselves across the rear of the fuselage to make sure the tail remained on the ground, and that the aircraft did not tip forward on to its nose.

[38]

After one RAF fighter pilot had completed his run up and scrambled (taken off in a hurry), become airborne and started to climb, he found the aircraft was behaving oddly — flying distinctly tail-heavy. After making quick adjustments on the tail-trimming device to bring the nose down, the aircraft was still tail-heavy. Then, as he glanced in the mirror, he discovered the reason. One of the ground crew, a WAAF (a member of the Women's Auxiliary Air Force) was still clinging to the tail, sprawled across the rear of the fuselage. Had there been a *Guinness Book of Records* in those days, they would have been in it. Both kept calm, with the pilot easing the aircraft gently round in a circuit back to base to make a perfect landing, without harm to either.

Under normal circumstances the ground crew would have stepped clear after the roar of the engines (during the run up to full throttle on the ground) had subsided, together with the force of the slip stream and vibration. However the transition into take-off had been so quick that the young lady had no time to let go. If she had, once the aircraft was rolling forward, she could have been knocked out or killed by the tail as it passed over her. 'Chocks away' gained a new urgency after that incident whenever anyone wanted 'to get cracking'.

Choice *see* You PAYS your money and you takes your choice

Choice *see* HOBSON'S CHOICE

It's a cinch is an American expression for anything that is really easy, or a certainty. It came into use at the end of the 19th century, but didn't become widely used in Britain until more recent times.

When the Spaniards landed on the coast of Mexico, in 1519, they brought horses with them. Neither these animals nor cows had been seen by the native Indians, and the sight of mounted men in armour appeared supernatural and terrified them. After a year or two, when the shock had been overcome, cowboys and cattle were plentiful and became accepted. Over the centuries they spread northwards to the American West.

The Mexican saddles needed to be strong to cope with the stress of roping cattle, as well as comfortable for continuous day-long use. Among the special features of the saddles, which were highly decorative, was a large horn on the raised front of the saddle, to which the rounded up and roped cattle could be attached. The other vital feature was the 'cincha' (equivalent to the 'girth' on modern riding saddles) which was adopted later by the early American pioneers and cowboys, and called the 'cinch'.

The cinch, which was wide and strong, could be tightened so that it was certain to remain secure, in the same way that 'It's a cinch' is a certainty, or 'sure thing'.

The coast is clear To check that 'the coast is clear' is to make sure that no one is around to witness or interfere with secret, or illicit, operations. The phrase originated during the heyday of smuggling which was not only lucrative, but a way of life, particularly for Devon and Cornish folk, and others living on or near Britain's southern coastline nearest to the Continent. Although the smuggling of these times has since been depicted as romantic, in reality there were often fierce and bloody fights, often to the death, with coastguards and excisemen on the cliff-tops and in the coves.

Smugglers stopped at nothing to ensure that the coast remained clear of intruders and informers. They invented stories of phantom ships and lights, and enlarged on legends to frighten officialdom and outsiders away. Some of the phantom ship stories have a ring of truth about them as many people of repute are said to have witnessed their strange comings and goings. A few of the legends seem to be confirmed though no one can offer any scientific or even plausible explanation.

The prize for sheer ingenuity must surely go to a band of Wiltshire smugglers. Getting barrels of spirits over considerable distances to towns inland called for journeys under the cover of darkness, and barrels were hidden in cellars, churchyards and village ponds during the daytime. On one occasion, the excisemen came upon villagers raking a village pond. They were smugglers trying to recover their spoils for the next stage of the journey but without any sign of panic on the arrival of the excisemen, the smugglers pretended to be village idiots and raked the pond around the reflection of the moon, which they explained had fallen from the sky, and which they were trying to recover.

Greatly amused at such an implausible explanation the excisemen rode away to continue their patrol, and the nickname of 'moonraker' was applied thereafter to simpletons.

Clothes line *see* SLEEP on a clothes line

A wolf in sheep's clothing is someone pretending to be what they are not, sometimes in disguise, usually for gain or greed. Apart from the wolf in Aesop's fable, there are many modern examples that most people can think of, but one little-known illustration of the saying comes from the story of how the first machine for the manufacture of raw silk came to be

[40]

erected in England, in 1719. It is a story which has a flavour of industrial espionage about it, which proves that this activity is anything but modern in origin.

The process was secret, the Italians having possessed the knowledge exclusively, with the most severe laws being brought in to preserve it. A high-spirited young Englishman named Lombe was determined, nonetheless, to become master of the secret and he managed to disguise himself in one of the Italian factories as a worker dressed in the meanest attire. In time, he was engaged to superintend a spinning engine, and eventually to sleep in the mill. But he took very little sleep for, with the aid of matches and a dark lantern, he took drawings of every important part of the machinery, forwarded them to his brother, Sir Thomas Lombe in Derby, England, and then made his escape.

Lombe's departure excited suspicion, and it was thought of such importance that an Italian vessel was sent in pursuit but he arrived safely in England. He did not see his mill in operation, though. He died prematurely, of slow poison, believed to have been administered by a person employed for the purpose by his enemies in Italy.

On cloud nine — Cloud-cuckoo-land Since ancient times the number nine (and three) has been of special significance, and also appears frequently in folklore. Nine, being a multiple of three is usually lucky. To be 'ON CLOUD NINE' is to be supremely happy (*see* 'Over the MOON'). The original phrase was 'on cloud seven', referring to the 'seventh heaven', or a state of total bliss and contentment. Astrologers held that there were seven planets which governed the universe and the life of man, the seventh heaven being the highest and the abode of God.

CLOUD CUCKOO LAND, on the other hand, relates to an unreal or imaginary situation, or state of affairs, which bears no relation to real life. Referring to an imaginary city built in the air by the birds in one of the comedies by Aristophanes (*c.*448–385 BC), one of the great dramatists of ancient Greece.

In 1516, Sir Thomas More, the English statesman, scholar and author, wrote a romance *Utopia* in Latin which was translated into English in 1551. Utopia (like 'cloud cuckoo land') which means 'nowhere' was the name of an imaginary island in More's book of that name, which represents the abode of a perfect and happy society, free from all worries and miseries, with an ideal social and political system, in which all are equal and everyone free to worship as they choose. No one is allowed to become rich through the oppression of others; everything is under communal ownership, and everyone is duty bound to perform an

[41]

equal amount of work. Utopia, as a result, refers to a place, or state of affairs, in which everything is perfect for everyone.

If something is described as Utopian in the present-day this implies an impracticable or idealistic scheme for the improvement of society.

To be in clover is to be content, at ease and in luxury, altogether in a thoroughly favourable situation or position. It is derived from the contentment of farm animals when offered such a delectable plant as fodder, which is so rich in proteins and minerals.

According to ancient superstition, all clovers possess the magical properties of providing protection and bringing good luck to human beings. Anyone who discovered one of the rare four-leaved clovers could count on exceptional good fortune.

Join the club When someone recounts and experience to a group of people which he believes to be unique, he may be greeted with the phrase 'join the club'. The people are implying that they have been, or are, in a similar position. The phrase similarly applies when someone has a grievance; the person complaining finds that everyone he knows has suffered in a similar manner, and that they all share the same point of view.

The word 'club', which comes from the old English 'clubbe', refers to an association of people, bound by some common interest, who meet for social purposes to exchange views, and have drinks and meals together. Originally, the groups met at taverns or coffee-houses and one of the first clubs founded in London was that established in the early 1600s at the Mermaid Tavern, in Friday Street, which included Shakespeare and Sir Walter Raleigh among its members.

Coffee-houses also supplied ale, beer, and tea and by the end of the 17th century there were no fewer than 2,000 such premises in London alone. An admission fee of twopence was made to these comfortable surroundings where men could sit and read newspapers, talk with friends and new acquaintances, discuss politics and other topics; and enjoy drink and food, which they had to pay for, of course. They could also use the premises as an address from which to despatch and receive letters. Samuel Pepys was a great frequenter of coffee-houses, belonging to the clubs that met in them, and in the taverns.

By 1764, Dr Samuel Johnson had founded his famous Literary Club which included like-minded men of varied talents, such as the great actor Garrick, Joshua Reynolds, the painter, the playwrights Goldsmith and

Sheridan, and biographer Boswell. The coffee-houses established the London clubs as we know them today.

Dr Johnson so enjoyed these opportunities for close association with other people, the convivial atmosphere, good company and discussion, that he said, 'I look upon every day to be lost, in which I do not make a new acquaintance.' London's oldest club, White's in St James', had already been founded around seventy years earlier, so had Boodles; Brooks was founded later. Clubs continued to meet in coffee-houses and taverns and did not occupy their own premises until the early 19th century.

The last word on clubs should go to Charles Dickens, who described the House of Commons, in one of his novels, as the best club in London. As he was a reporter at one time, and regarded as the most accurate reporter in the Commons gallery, he spoke from personal experience. There are many engaged in politics today who would agree with him.

I haven't a clue means that one has no idea of the answer to a question, or has no knowledge at all of the subject under discussion. A clue is a ball of thread (*cleowen* in old English), something which serves as a guide, or suggests a way of solving a problem, as illustrated in the celebrated Greek legend of the Cretan Labyrinth.

The labyrinth, which was constructed of intricate, winding, under- ground passages, was not only vast and an easy place in which to become lost, it also contained the dreaded Minotaur, which was half- man and half-bull, imprisoned there by Minos, king of Crete. Each year Minos demanded a tribute of seven youths and seven maidens to be devoured by the monster. When the great hero Theseus, son of the king of Athens, arrived in Crete and heard of this appalling sacrifice he immediately offered himself as one of the victims, believing that it was within his power to slay the monster.

The Cretan king's daughter fell in love with Theseus and gave him the means by which he might be saved — a sword, with which to kill the monster, and a skein of thread by means of which he could find his way out of the labyrinth where the monster was kept.

Excavations, in comparatively recent years, have uncovered the remains of the vast palace of King Minos which are so intricate in design and layout that they suggest a skein of thread would have provided the only clue to finding a way out of the labyrinth.

The labyrinth had been built by Daedalus for King Minos, who showed his gratitude by imprisoning him, and his son Icarus, in the palace. Besides being a builder, Daedalus was an inventor who set about making two sets of wings so that he and his son could escape. When the time came for take-off, Daedalus warned his son not to fly too high. As they flew out of prison Daedalus made a safe landing in Sicily, but Icarus was so exhilarated that he climbed higher and higher to enjoy the new experience of flight. So high, in fact, that the sun melted the wax holding the feathers of his wings together, and he fell into the sea.

Man has always envied the birds and wanted to fly — but Icarus, was over-enthusiastic and, to coin a modern phrase, 'clueless'.

Coat *see* To TURN one's coat

A cobbler should stick to his last is advice not to interfere in matters about which you know little or nothing, particularly in relation to other people's trades, or professions.

The cobbler, of the 4th century BC is said to have noticed a fault in a shoe-latchet in a painting by the most celebrated Greek painter, Apelles. After the artist had rectified the error, the cobbler had the audacity to criticize the legs, whereupon Apelles put the cobbler in his place by telling him, 'Keep to your trade — you understand about shoes, but not about anatomy.'

Pliny, the Roman historian summed it up centuries later when he wrote: *Ne supra crepidam sutor iudicaret* . . . the cobbler should not judge beyond his last.

A cock and bull story is a long, rambling, tale which is so incredible that few are prepared to believe it. The origin of the phrase is thought by some to come from the old fables in which cocks, bulls and other animals conversed in human language. But another suggestion is that it has been handed down from the old coaching days, when gossip and stories heard in one inn. The Cock, were retold in another nearby inn, The Bull, and exaggerated in the process.

According to Cocker (or Gunter) means correct, and exactly as it should be, with no possibility of a mistake. Both gentlemen were English mathematicians. Edmund Gunter (1581–1626) was responsible for methods of solving problems in surveying and navigation. He invented the 'chain', which was 66 ft long (20.117 m) and divided into 100 links, used as a measurement of length in land surveying, and a flat rule with scales (known as 'Gunter's Scale') which was used to solve mathematical problems mechanically.

Edward Cocker (1631–1675) became famous for the textbook *Arith-*

metick which was so popular that it ran into 112 editions, and it was this 'exact' work which gave rise to the saying 'according to Cocker'. Americans tend to use the alternative phrase 'according to Gunter'.

Colours *see* To sail under FALSE colours

Concert pitch *see* To SCREW oneself up to concert pitch

As bald as a coot — Crazy as a coot The common Coot, which is a water bird 15–18 inches long (38–46 cm) has a white bill which extends to form a conspicuous white plate on the forehead, which has given it the name of 'bald coot'. The phrase, of 15th-century origin, arose from this bald-headed appearance which is particularly prominent against its sooty black plumage.

Coots are shy birds normally preferring quiet ponds and more isolated areas, but in winter they can often be seen in large numbers on lakes, reservoirs and estuaries. They tend to squabble and fly at one another for no apparent reason which accounts for the other phrase 'as crazy as a coot', used to describe anyone who behaves in an odd and erratic manner.

Course *see* Only the FIRST course

Courses *see* HORSES for courses

To send someone to Coventry This familiar phrase refers to a form of punishment inflicted by a group of people, who refuse to speak or associate with someone who has offended them, or broken some rule. It dates from the time of the English Civil War of the 17th century, when Coventry was a Parliamentary stronghold. The soldiers of the king were so disliked by the citizens that Royalist prisoners, captured in Birmingham and other towns, were sent to Coventry, where it was known that the people would ignore them, not speak to them, and carry on as if they were not there.

It's not cricket When this is said to anyone, or of anything, it means that something is unfair, contrary to fair play, or 'not playing the game'. Although cricket existed as a well-organized sport in England as long ago as 1344, the villagers of Boxgrove, near the cathedral city of Chichester in Sussex, were probably the first to say 'It's not cricket' when they were prosecuted for playing the game on a Sunday, in 1622.

[45]

It is no use crying over spilt milk This originated in the mid-17th century and points out the uselessness of bemoaning the past; whatever has happened, has happened, and there is nothing we can do about it now. It is not easy advice to follow because everyone has regrets.

Ella Wheeler Wilcox, the popular American writer of verses, provides us with some comfort, however, in her poem *Solitude* written in 1883 which revived and enlarged on another saying which had been in everyday use long before then when she wrote:

> Laugh, and the world laughs with you;
> Weep, and you weep alone;
> For the sad old earth must borrow its mirth,
> But has trouble enough of its own.

If neither of these sayings bring comfort we can, perhaps, cry over spilt milk after all; and weep, even if we weep alone. For, according to recent American medical research it is not weak to cry, and tears can do us good, banish worries, help dispel frustrations, and even improve our general health.

Curtain *see* A curtain LECTURE

To cut and run In the late 17th century seamen would often threaten to cut someone's painter, to prevent them from doing any mischief. (The painter is the rope attached to the bow of a ship for making it fast.) Two centuries later, to get rid of anyone, sailors would tell them 'to cut and run', meaning cut their painter, and make off.

The phrase 'to cut and run' when used earlier also meant to sever a connection, but to do so in order to escape in a hurry, such as when a ship was at anchor and about to be attacked by an approaching enemy. The anchor 'cable' in those days was made of hemp, so could be cut.

The sword of Damocles is an expression used to convey uncertainty, or impending danger in the midst of prosperity. Damocles, who was one of the courtiers of Dionysius the Elder of Syracuse, in Sicily, in the 4th century BC, made the mistake of extolling the king's fortune by saying how happy he must be as ruler amidst such splendour.

The tyrant king laid on a sumptuous banquet which Damocles enjoyed until he realised he was being taught a lesson. For, when he looked up, he saw a sword hanging by a single hair above his head — placed there to typify the uncertainty of a ruler's life.

Meeting a deadline The original 'deadline' referred to a line, or space limit, marked out some distance from the fence of a prisoner-of-war camp during the American Civil War. Any prisoner crossing it was likely to be shot on sight.

The 'deadline' in this expression today refers to a date or time by which something must be completed. Writers and artists invariably have to work to a deadline, as so many other people and operations are subsequently involved in the presentation of their work — this involves a tight schedule and detailed planning. Anyone who fails to meet a deadline is liable to throw the whole process into confusion.

Between the devil and the deep sea Anyone in this situation is faced with a dilemma, or two dangers of equal peril. The phrase comes from classical Greek mythology and refers to the treacherous waters near the narrow Straits of Messina, between Sicily and Italy, through which the galleys of Odysseus had to pass.

On one side, there was the dreaded sea-monster Scylla whose six heads were capable of reaching out from her cave and seizing six crew members at a time from the decks. On the other side, there was the terrifying cliff of Charybdis on which another fearful monster lived. The monster sucked in the sea and then poured it out in a giant whirlpool, three times a day, hurling ships and crews to ruin, from which there was no escape.

The devil to pay This phrase indicates trouble ahead, and it came into use during the time of the old sailing ships. The 'devil' was a long seam next to the keel of a ship which had to be paid (sealed) with tar. If there was no hot pitch ready the tide would turn before the work could be done and the ship would be out of commission for much longer than necessary.

What the dickens? has nothing to do with Charles Dickens, the 19th-century English novelist. Shakespeare had made use of the phrase long before in *The Merry Wives of Windsor.* (Mrs Page says of Falstaff, 'I cannot tell what the dickens his name is . . .') In those times the word 'dickens' was used in preference to 'devil' which was considered impolite; though, today, modern playwrights might well write: 'I can't remember what the hell his name is'.

Dilemma *see* on the HORNS of a dilemma

As dull as ditchwater This phrase has been used for well over 200 years; the dull colour of the muddy water is likened to people who are uninteresting, as well as to jobs which are tedious.

What is dull to one person, however, is often of interest to another. Ditchwater when studied under a microscope by a naturalist can be seen to contain a vast number of minute living things, from plants to animals, which are full of fascination. Few people had access to a microscope when the phrase originated, though, and it has remained in use.

Do as you would be done by The Earl of Chesterfield (1694–1773) the English statesman, author, and patron of literature wrote a whole series of letters to his son, full of worldly wisdom and practical advice including, 'Do as you would be done by is the surest method that I know of pleasing'. It was inspired by a 14th-century proverb which, in turn, later inspired Charles Kingsley (1819–1875), the English clergyman and author, to invent the fearsome lady, Mrs Bedonebyasyoudid, in his delightful book for children, *The Water Babies.*

In another letter he wrote: 'It is an undoubted truth, that the less one has to do, the less time one finds to do it in. One yawns, one procrastinates, one can do it when one will, and therefore one seldom does it at all'.

Although Charles Kingsley stammered in ordinary conversation, he never did so when he was preaching or praying. In modern times there have been many instances where male or female stammerers have been able to recite poetry before an audience in clear-cut tones without the slightest impediment in their speech. But when resorting to ordinary conversation again the hesitancy and difficulties return. If anyone were to laugh at them it would be in bad taste and hurtful — we would certainly not like it if we had their handicap and were ridiculed because of it. If the advice in the proverb to 'Do as you would be done by' were universally followed, it would provide the recipe for a near-perfect world.

There are many proverbs which tell us what we should and should not do, such as . . .

'Do as I say, not as I do'
'Do as you're bidden and you'll never bear blame'
'Never put off till tomorrow what may be done today'
'What may be done at any time is done at no time'

Samuel Rogers (1763–1855) who published several volumes of poems at his own expense, but declined the poet laureateship when Wordsworth died, took things further when he wrote, 'Think nothing done while aught remains to do'.

No can do — Can do — Will do These phrases would appear to be comparatively modern ones, but the first two were in regular use in the Royal Navy from around 1850 onwards. In civilian life, all three were commonly used in everyday speech in recent times to let someone know that one either could or could not do a job, keep an appointment, or meet their request. The phrases are now used much less, and servicemen and civilians tend to shorten them to 'negative' or 'affirmative'. In the USA they also use 'no dice' for 'nothing doing'.

As dead as a dodo means something which is dead, extinct, or long out of fashion. The dodo was a large flightless bird, which became extinct in the 1680s.

The dodo, which was heavily built, clumsy, and totally unable to fly or defend itself, belonged to a species which lived on the island of Mauritius in the Indian Ocean. Although it was not hunted to any great extent for meat by the sailors who visited the island, the seafarers were instrumental in bringing about its extinction, as well as that of its close relative the solitaire (also called Dodo) which lived on the Réunion and nearby Rodriguez islands. Pigs were introduced (and, accidentally, rats) to the islands to ensure that other seamen visiting the areas would have a supply of meat. As the pigs (and rats) roamed free they destroyed the dodo's nests, eggs and young, which reduced breeding to such an extent that it led to the dodo's extinction.

The dodo had a round, fat body, bigger than a turkey's, a large head with a great hooked bill, short wings, a small tail of curly feathers, and short stubby legs which could scarcely support its weight. Its appearance has become known from drawings, relics of stuffed specimens, and a number of skeletons dug up on the islands.

Sir John Tenniel's well-known bird illustrations for *Alice in Wonderland* which included the dodo were based on the drawings of artists who were able to draw the bird from life. One of the few artists who painted a living specimen, however, made the mistake of giving the dodo two right legs. Subsequent artists copied this original painting, and each other and, thus, repeated the error for three centuries.

Dog days

'Youth will be served, every dog has his day, and mine has been a fine one.'

George Borrow
(1803–1881)

Poets and authors, including Shakespeare and Charles Kingsley, have included the phrase 'every dog has his day' in their writings through the centuries. Today, when we speak of 'dog days' we are referring to the hottest days of the year, during the month of July and first half of August, which were believed in ancient times to be under the influence of Sirius, the dog star.

Sirius is the brightest star we see, because it is closer than most other stars, even though it is eight-and-a-half light years away.

In ancient Egypt the sighting of Sirius marked the beginning of the new year. Priests were in charge of the calendar, and in one of their temples, in which the aisle was lined with tall columns, the statue of a goddess was placed at the end so that the light of the returning dog star would fall upon a jewel, on her forehead, and make it shine. The moment it did so they were able to announce the beginning of the new year.

Dog *see* A HAIR of the dog that bit you

Dog in the manger is used to describe the attitude of someone who stops others from using something that he does not himself want, but is determined to prevent others from using it.

It comes from Aesop's fable about a dog which made a habit of lying in a manger. Although he could not eat the hay, he growled and snarled at the oxen and horses every time they came near the manger, thus denying them what he could not use himself.

Aesop, who lived from about 620 to 560 BC, did not write his fables, but recited them, and they were handed down from memory. Two centuries passed before anyone wrote them down as they were then told. Another collection followed, some time later, compiled by a Greek named Babrius. The stories were lost to memory for a thousand years afterwards, until 1844 AD when a copy of Babrius' collection was discovered in the monastery of Mt Athos.

Top-dog, under-dog Before the days of electric saw mills, all timber had to be cut by hand. Logs from felled trees were placed over pits specially dug in the ground and two men using a long saw cut the timber. One man (the bottom sawyer) stood in the pit and, as he had the worst job and got covered in sawdust, he came to be known as the 'under-dog'. The more fortunate man (the top sawyer) stood above the pit at ground level and guided the saw as it cut, and was called the 'top-dog'.

In the doghouse When dogs misbehaved themselves they were traditionally relegated to their kennel outside the house. Anyone who finds himself 'in the doghouse' today is similarly in disgrace. The saying is usually applied to a husband who has upset his wife in some way by doing, or not doing, something.

Members of motor racing's Doghouse Club, however, are anything but in disgrace. Since it was founded in Britain around a quarter of a century ago, it has raised large sums of money each year for charities. It came into being when a group of wives of internationally famous Grand Prix drivers, world champions amongst them, became exasperated with their husbands' behaviour in getting up from dinner tables in hotels, and at dinner dances, to huddle in a corner talking shop, leaving the wives sitting alone at their different tables around the room. The drivers were put 'in the doghouse'. When they learnt about the formation of the club, however, they backed its fund-raising activities to the hilt, and still do so to this day.

In the doldrums Anyone who finds himself in this state is down in the dumps and depressed, usually because nothing is happening, and everything seems black and unlikely to change.

Christopher Columbus and his crew knew what it was like to be 'in the doldrums' when they were becalmed for so many weeks before reaching

America. The doldrums are the region of calms near the equator; they are darkened with clouds from the moisture gathered by the north and south trade winds on each side. Ships are becalmed in them and crews become demoralized.

Donkey work Anyone asked to carry out 'the donkey work' can expect to find themselves engaged on dull, repetitive work.

Donkeys have been used for many tasks, from carrying people and goods, to drawing the water from wells. At Carisbrooke Castle, on the Isle of Wight, the well water was drawn up, originally, by the prisoners of the castle. Each time the bucket was raised to the surface, the prisoner had walked the equivalent of 300 yards (274 metres). During the past hundred years the tread-wheel has been worked by donkeys. It takes six months to train each donkey and, although such work seems monotonous to us, they appear to thrive on it. One of them, it is recorded, lived to the ripe old age of forty-nine years.

Donkey's years usually refers to a very long passage of time since one did something or saw someone. The phrase is probably derived from a word-play on 'donkey's ears' which are very long. An alternative expression for a long time, which is often used today, is 'yonks ago' or 'yonks years', from the sound made by a donkey.

A baker's dozen In the Middle Ages, bakers suffered severe penalties if they sold loaves of bread which were below the legal weight. To avoid prosecution for any unintentional sale below this standard the bakers added an extra loaf free to every twelve, so 'a baker's dozen' is really thirteen.

Thirteen is regarded as an unlucky number by many people. The superstition is said to have arisen because thirteen were present at the Last Supper but, although it existed far earlier in pagan times, it is still considered unlucky for thirteen people to sit together at the dining-table.

For bakers thirteen was perhaps an unlucky number as the Great Fire of London, in 1666, is alleged to have started as a result of a spark from the oven of Charles II's baker, Thomas Farrinor, in Pudding Lane. He had checked the oven before retiring to bed, but was awoken after midnight by fire, smoke, and fumes coming upstairs. He and his family managed to escape through a window to the adjoining house, but the housemaid, who was overcome, with vertigo and fright, perished and became the first victim of the fire. It spread quickly, destroying 13,200 houses in four days, and made over 100,000 people homeless. Surprisingly, only eight people were reported to have lost their lives as a direct result of the fire.

Nineteen to the dozen When this expression is applied to speech, it refers to anyone who talks incessantly. It originated in Cornish copper and tin mines at the time when steam-powered pumping engines were introduced, in the 1770s, to overcome the considerable difficulties experienced with flooding.

The pumps were patented and the users had to pay premiums to the makers, based on the savings which the pumps effected. One report of the time stated that one of the mines had got 'nineteen to the dozen', indicating that it had raised 19,000 gallons (86,376 litres) of water for every twelve bushels (436 cu. m.) of coal used.

Drink *see* To drink a TOAST

Drink *see* Eat, drink, and be MERRY

To be drummed out *see* To be BOWLER-HATTED

Drunk as a lord For centuries men have boasted about the amount of alcohol they can consume at a sitting. Some can take their drink well, others not. Exactly why the nobility should have been picked out and labelled for their over-indulgence is not clear. Those who say that only lords could afford excessive drinking overlook the fact that during the first half of the 18th century, for instance, more gin was drunk by people of all classes of Britain than at any other time. More than 100,000 people in London alone drank gin, when it was possible to get drunk for one penny, and dead drunk for twopence. Inevitably, there was lawlessness and violence. Reforms, licences, and a duty, were introduced by Parliament to control the consumption. The duty led to tax evasion, and idleness and social difficulties continued until a new Act, passed in the mid-18th century, improved matters and reduced the worst excesses of drunkenness and over-indulgence.

'Drunk as a lord', was a phrase in everyday use in the mid-17th century, but so was 'drunk as a beggar', though only the former remained popular and survived to this day.

An ugly duckling When this phrase is used in its widest sense, it can refer to anything which appears unpromising at first, but which turns into something much better in the course of time. Originally, it was applied to a dull or ordinary child that develops into an attractive and interesting adult. The phrase comes from Hans Christian Andersen's story, *The Ugly Duckling*. The duck's foster mother was greatly surprised when the ungainly little creature she had looked after (which was really a cygnet) grew up into a beautiful, graceful, swan.

Down in the dumps To be 'down in the dumps' is to be in a depressed and melancholy frame of mind. This is something which afflicts young and old alike, and people of all temperaments. It is mentioned in an early nursery rhyme. Shakespeare used the expression 'in the dumps' in *The Taming of the Shrew* when referring to the high-spirited and fiery tempered Katharine, who normally relieved her pent up feelings, before they had time to gain hold of her, by resorting to actions such as crashing her lute down on the head of her music-master when he had had the effrontery to find fault with her performance.

'Dumps' has a close association with the Dutch word *dompig*, which means dull or low.

To earmark is to set something aside for a particular purpose — the phrase coming from the old custom of putting marks on the ears of cattle and sheep to denote their ownership. Today we might 'earmark' some funds for a definite purpose, for instance, but in the Bible the process was applied to people. In Exodus 21: 6, we read '. . . and his master shall bore his ear through with an aul; and he shall serve him for ever'.

To have burning or itching ears According to an old superstition, if your ears are burning it means that someone is talking about you. If the sensation is felt in the right ear, it means that they are speaking well of you, whereas if it is the left ear, it implies that the talk is unfavourable.

Itching ears denote a hankering to hear some item of news, scandal or gossip. Hence the expression 'I'm itching to hear' which comes from a passage in the Bible from 2 Timothy 4: 3–4, 'For the time will come when they will not endure sound doctrine; but after their own lusts shall they heap to themselves teachers, having itching ears; And they shall turn away *their* ears from the truth, and shall be turned unto fables'.

Walls have ears is a warning that others might be listening when matters that are secret are being discussed. The phrase was used widely during World War II, along with others such as 'Careless talk costs lives', and 'Be like dad, keep mum!'

The warning is supposed to have been coined in the time of Catherine de Medici, who learnt of State secrets, and plots by listening through the walls of certain rooms.

Eat *see* Eat, drink, and be MERRY

Eat *see* To eat HUMBLE PIE

An eavesdropper is someone who places himself in a favourable position, without being noticeable, so that he can listen to what other people are saying. The expression is an old one, and refers to the parts of the roof which project beyond the walls, and throw off the rain water. The space of ground around the house on which this rain water fell was known as the eavesdrop, and anyone who stood within this area close to the house to overhear what was being said inside was called an 'eavesdropper'. Nowadays, it refers more generally to anyone who listens to other people's conversation, indoors or in the open, without being seen or noticed.

Don't put all your eggs in one basket This phrase, originating in the 18th century, suggests that it is unwise to risk everything on a single venture. In other words, it is better to spread one's time, money, or efforts in several different directions as a safeguard against possible disappointment or ruin. Then, if the unexpected happens, or if anything fails, you will have other means to fall back on.

Like the curate's egg means that something is good, or satisfactory, in some ways, though not in others.

The phrase arose from an illustrated joke in one of the 1895 issues of *Punch* magazine in which a curate is taking breakfast in the home of his bishop who says, 'I'm afraid you've got a bad egg, Mr Jones.' As the curate continues to dip his spoon into the egg, he looks across at the Bishop and says: 'Oh no, my Lord, I assure you! Parts of it are excellent.' Nowadays, critics often refer to a work or performance as being 'like the curate's egg — good in parts'.

As sure as eggs is eggs which means something is certain, and came into everyday use as a phrase during the 17th century, has nothing to do with eggs but is a corruption of the mathematical formula 'as sure as X is X'.

To have egg all over one's face On occasions when someone tends to 'egg one on' (urges one to do something), it is quite possible that one could end up by looking foolish with 'egg all over one's face'.

Don't teach your grandmother to suck eggs Eggs, which are the symbol of resurrection and continuing life, have been a subject of folklore and superstition for centuries, and still feature in many everyday phrases. The advice given in this one comes from the early 18th century and warns that one should not try to teach, or give advice to, anyone who is older and more experienced than oneself. The supposition is that as one's grandmother gave birth to one's mother who, in turn, gave birth to us, the grandmother is the most knowledgeable and, therefore, doesn't need advice.

Nest egg To have a 'nest egg' put by is an early 17th-century expression which refers to anyone who has saved some money. The allusion is to the pottery egg which used to be put into a hen's nest to induce her to lay her own eggs there. Thus, if a person saves some money, a start has been made which like the pottery egg, can then serve as an inducement for them to add to it.

A white elephant is an expression used to describe some expensive item, or possession, usually large, which turns out to be useless to its owner and is often costly to maintain, and difficult to get rid of. The phrase relates to the successive kings of Siam who gave a white elephant to any courtier who annoyed them. Although the animals were held in high esteem, and regarded as sacred, their upkeep was so costly that anyone who received one was inevitably ruined.

Face *see* Face the MUSIC

Fall between two stools This phrase comes from the Latin proverb 'between two stools one falls to the ground', and highlights the dangers that can arise through hesitation or indecision between two choices, or courses of action, which may be similar but which could have different results. A failure to make up one's mind one way or the other, or an attempt to achieve both aims at once, could land one in difficulties and result in missing out on both alternatives, thus achieving neither.

To sail under false colours is to use deception by assuming a false character in order to obtain some personal advantage, or being hypocritical in pretending to have certain beliefs or principles which one does not have. The phrase arose from the fact that pirate vessels tried to avoid detection by flying a false flag.

The pirate's flag, 'the Jolly Roger', with its white skull and cross-bones on a black background, was actually unknown during the early centuries of piracy. In spite of all that has been written about it since and the films that have been made, it did not come into use until the 18th century. During the 200 years up to the mid-18th century there were hundreds of pirates plundering wherever they roamed the world's oceans. By the early 19th century their power had been broken almost everywhere, except for an occasional junk or two which continued to plunder small craft in far-eastern waters.

Feast *see* To have a BEAN feast

Feast *see* SKELETON at the feast

A feather in your cap is an honour, award, or acknowledgement of an achievement which one has reason to be proud of.

It is sometimes attributed to the custom of American Indians (and others) who wore feathers as a sign of their bravery in war. The number of feathers worn in their headgear accounted for each enemy slain. The

[57]

more likely explanation for the phrase, however, comes from the slender, smooth, glossy black plume of the heron's crest which was deemed a mark of great distinction in medieval chivalry, and was used as the centre of the ostrich-white plume which adorned the caps of the noble Knights of the Garter.

Admiral Lord Nelson had a superb heron's plume presented to him by the Sultan of Persia, richly set in diamonds — the highest honour which could be conferred upon him.

On your feet was used mainly as a military command, meaning either stand up immediately, or get on at once with the work or duties that had to be performed. Its use in civilian life originated with the 'Hallelujah' chorus, from Handel's *Messiah*. When George II heard this he was so moved by it that he stood up to indicate his wonder and respect, starting a tradition which survives amongst audiences to this day.

Although Handel became blind in his later years, he still played and conducted his oratorios. He died a week after collapsing during a performance of the *Messiah* which he had been conducting.

To sit on the fence is to be neutral and to avoid taking sides in any conflict or dispute, not committing oneself in any way. An experienced fence-sitter waits to see who is going to win, or get the better of the argument, and then comes down on the right side of the fence to join the winner.

What a fiasco! is used to describe a complete failure of organization or workmanship, a breakdown in a performance, or some event or other. Two alternatives have been given as to the origin of the phrase both of which are Italian. *Fiasco* is the Italian for flask or bottle. The craftsmanship of the beautiful old Venetian glass is renowned the world over; when any flaw occurred in the blowing of a delicate piece it was abandoned, and turned into a common flask, a 'fiasco'.

The phrase was often shouted in Italian opera houses in the form of 'Olà, olà, fiasco!' when the audience expressed their disapproval of an unpopular singer, or one who sang a false note and failed to please them.

To fiddle while Rome burns — To play second fiddle — Fiddle about — To fiddle anything — On the fiddle — To have a face as long as a fiddle — Fiddle-faddle — Fiddlesticks — Fit as a fiddle It is strange that so beautiful an instrument as the violin, whose music gives such pleasure, should be associated with the word 'fiddle' which has given rise to so

[58]

many phrases with negative connotations. Things might have been different but for the Emperor Nero, who was said to have played an instrument and sung while he watched Rome burning, thus giving rise to the phrase TO FIDDLE WHILE ROME BURNS. The phrase is used to describe anyone who does nothing, or occupies himself with trifles, when faced with a crisis, or when something important is happening.

The stringed instrument Nero played in 64 AD was the lyre; the fire burnt for a week and destroyed more than half the city. The violin, as we know it, was not developed in Italy until the 16th century.

As the first violin leads the orchestra, the phrase TO PLAY SECOND FIDDLE, which became popular in the 19th century, is used to describe anyone who is playing or acting in a subordinate role. It usually applies to an unenviable task imposed on one. William Thackeray wrote in his novel *Pendennis*: '"I've played a second fiddle all through life" he said with a bitter laugh.'

'To play the fiddle' or FIDDLE ABOUT describes anyone who is idle, messes about, or fritters their time away. While TO FIDDLE ANYTHING or be ON THE FIDDLE, is to act dishonestly, especially when it comes to dealing with accounts, in order to gain some advantage. The last two phrases originated, presumably, from the busy fingers manipulating the strings of a violin.

TO HAVE A FACE AS LONG AS A FIDDLE is to look dismal. FIDDLE-FADDLE and FIDDLESTICKS are used as retorts to imply that what one is saying is nonsense. FIT AS A FIDDLE (one of the rare positive phrases involving 'fiddle') describes anyone in good form and fine spirits.

To be a fifth columnist was a phrase used widely during World War II to describe anyone who, while living or serving in one country and apparently working for it, was in fact a traitor acting in secret and doing all they could to assist its enemies. The expression originated during the Spanish Civil War (1936–1939) when the Fascist general attacking Madrid said that he had five columns in action: four were in position encircling the city, and a fifth column, consisting of people who were working for him, was secretly inside.

A figurehead is a nominal leader of an organization, or group of people, chosen to inspire confidence because of their status or social background, who serves in this capacity without any real authority and, often, without taking any active part in the proceedings.

The figurehead of any vessel is more than just a passenger or an ornament — sailors in the past regarded them with the greatest respect.

[59]

They believed the figurehead to embody the ship's soul, and to go to sea without one was considered highly dangerous. The early ships were dedicated to goddesses, which explains why the carved effigy, or figurehead, of a woman came to be fixed on the bows of vessels, also why ships are always regarded as feminine and referred to as 'she' or 'her'.

Keep your fingers crossed Fingers are linked with many superstitions, for instance, when we 'cross our fingers', while walking under a ladder, or we say to someone that we will keep our fingers crossed for them, we are, in effect, resorting to the ancient belief that this action will ward off misfortune, or ensure good luck against adversity or setbacks that might arise when something important is about to happen.

There are many expressions about fingers. Most people have let things 'slip through their fingers', or had something 'at their fingertips', or a 'finger in the pie', or 'pointed the finger at someone', or 'twisted them around their little finger'. The fingers of a clumsy person are described as 'all thumbs', while the exceptional person is said to have more wit (wisdom) in their little finger than in the whole body of anyone else.

Fingers have also been associated through the ages with powers of healing. The third finger of the left hand was believed to have a very special and direct link with the heart, which explains why this finger is chosen on which to wear the wedding ring. It was also claimed that if a wound was stroked with the healing powers of this finger, a cure would soon be effected.

Fingers were made before forks This phrase has been in existence for centuries and is still used as an excuse, today, when someone is criticized for eating anything in their fingers instead of using a fork.

The Greeks did not have forks, nor do forks appear to have been used at table during any period of Roman history. In fact, their first use appears to have been at the table of 'John the Good', Duke of Burgundy, in the 14th century, and he had only two. At that time the loaves were round; they were cut into slices which were piled by the side of the carver. He had a pointed carving-knife, and a skewer of gold or silver, which he stuck into the joint; and having cut off a slice he placed it on a piece of bread which was served to the guest.

A leg or haunch of mutton had a piece of paper wrapped round the shank which the carver took hold of with one hand as he carved the joint with the other, and this is how the custom of ornamental hams with cut paper came into being.

Queen Elizabeth I was the first English sovereign to use a table fork, but they did not come into general use in England until the early 17th century. Even then it was considered a piece of affectation to use them in preference to fingers.

Only the first course means that something has only just begun and that there is something much more interesting, or important, to come. The saying is similar to the other popular one 'That's only for starters' which is also used today.

An early example of the use of this phrase might be the entertainment laid on by Cleopatra for her favourite, Mark Antony, which she declared would cost a fortune. Everything appeared to be costly and magnificent at their feast, yet there was nothing which could cost that much. As Mark Antony began to joke and point this out, Cleopatra commanded him to be patient: 'What you see', she said, 'is only the first course'.

As she gave a signal, two richly dressed boys brought her a magnificent vase studded with diamonds, which contained a strong vinegar. Cleopatra immediately took off one of her magnificent pearl ear-rings and threw it into the vase, and watched with delight at the apparent gradual melting of the precious jewel. After which, gracefully drinking the health of Mark Antony, she swallowed the costly draught. The value of Cleopatra's ear-rings was recorded by Pliny as being worth the equivalent of £52,000 *each*.

A similar act of extravagance was recorded during the reign of Elizabeth I, when Sir Thomas Gresham gave a sumptuous banquet for her at the opening of the Royal Exchange in London. He reduced a costly pearl to powder, mixed it in a goblet of wine, and drank it to the health of his royal guest.

A bunch of fives — A fourpenny one A blow from a fist, in which the fingers and thumb are compressed tightly inwards, was often called A BUNCH OF FIVES.

The actual blow struck against someone was often called A FOURPENNY ONE, which stems from the days when the wound suffered by a victim was carefully measured and the culprit was fined at the rate of a penny an inch.

The extent of an injury inflicted by a blow, or blows, is nowadays sometimes expressed in the number of stitches needed to heal the wound.

Best foot forward According to ancient superstition, held by people of many different races, any journey or start to a new enterprise or undertaking should be begun with the right foot (i.e. 'the best foot

[61]

forward'). If the left foot is used, the consequences are likely to be unfortunate.

The left-hand side, and the left foot, were considered unlucky, and this also applied to dressing. If the Romans made the mistake of putting on their left sandal first, they believed that it would lead to bad luck. Augustus Caesar is said to have attributed the mutiny of his soldiers to the fact that he put on his left sandal before the right on that particular morning.

The right foot should also be used first when entering a house, or church. Moslems leave their slippers at the door of the mosque, as a mark of respect, and enter with the right foot first over the threshold.

In England, the right foot is put forward first by brides as they enter the church, and the custom still persists today. In earlier times an old shoe was thrown at the bride and bridegroom as they departed from the reception for their honeymoon to bring them good luck. This led, later, to the custom of tying an old shoe to their horse-drawn carriage, and subsequently their motor-car.

To put one's foot in it When walking it is, of course, necessary to look where we are going. Similarly, when we say or do anything which affects others we need to think first, otherwise we are liable 'to put our foot in it', or blunder by doing or saying something which we regret afterwards, especially when it worsens the situation. The phrase is also used of someone who rushes in, without thinking, and says something stupid or inappropriate, thus committing a *faux pas* which compromises their own, or someone else's, reputation.

The phrase is an old one. During the 13th and 14th centuries people were likely to 'put their foot in it' in more ways than one, not only in what they said but because of the shoes they wore. These were adorned with such long peaks, turning upwards from the toe, that they had to be fastened by silver chains (or laces) to the knees. During Edward IV's reign (1461–1483) all finely dressed gentlemen looked as if they had the gout, for they wore cloth and velvet shoes so broad that their feet looked like great platters. Both types of shoes, long and broad, were awkward and cumbersome, also very wasteful of material. A law had to be introduced which limited the length of the peaks, and the width was limited to not more than 6 inches (15 cm) across the toes.

To hold the fort is to be in charge and keep things going while others, normally responsible are absent. The phrase is best known for its use, in 1864, during the American Civil War, when General Sherman signalled to General Corse, from the top of Kennesaw, 'Hold the fort, at all costs'.

To be a freelance is to act on one's own judgement, and be an independent person. Originally, the phrase came from the free companies of mercenary soldiers who roamed over Europe in the Middle Ages and were willing to sell their services to any cause or master. This meant, in effect, that they not only offered themselves but their lances for hire.

Nowadays, the term 'freelance' refers to artists, journalists, writers, musicians and any other skilled people who are not on the salaried staff of any organization, but self-employed, who sell their talents on the free market to those willing to pay.

French *see* To take French LEAVE

To frog march *see* To read the RIOT Act

A frog in the throat This expression is frequently used to describe anyone with a croaking voice or who is afflicted with hoarseness.

In the Middle Ages frogs were actually put into throats, not to be eaten but to cure infections, such as the fungus growth, known as 'thrush'. The head of a live frog was placed in the mouth and, as it breathed, it was said to withdraw the disease into itself.

The gift of the gab Anyone who has this talks a lot. What they say may be nonsense, childish, or even boastful! Alternatively, it may denote a considerable talent — an ability to have a full grasp, or understanding, of a particular subject and be able to speak fluently about it.

The word *gab* is connected with the word *gob*, meaning mouth, and is found in similar forms in many other European languages. The Old French *gobe* means a mouthful.

The name of the game — Quiz — Sixty-four-thousand-dollar question 'The name of the game' is the nub of the matter, or the vital issue. This is a phrase now used widely by politicians, trade union officials, and the public at large. Football managers often use it during team talks, and interviews with the press and television, when making an important point. This expression is of recent origin, but the word 'quiz', which means to enquire or question, came into use in 1780 in an odd way that prompted questions itself, and subsequently gave way to a new game.

At that time, just over 200 years ago, a Dublin theatre manager, a Mr Daly, laid a wager that he would introduce a new word into the language, within 24 hours. When he came up with 'quiz' the word was immediately chalked up on walls everywhere in the city and, as people did not know what it meant, everyone was soon discussing and questioning it.

'To quiz' someone, or question them, soon dropped into everyday use. During the past fifty years it has found its way into question and answer, and general knowledge, games or 'quiz shows' on radio, and subsequently television. In the dictionary the word 'quiz' used to refer to an odd or eccentric person, or hoaxer. The original hoaxer, Mr Daly, could have made a fortune if he had thought of inviting audiences to quiz shows in his theatre. Today they are listened to and watched by millions all over the world.

One of the most popular original radio quiz programmes was that in America in which the last and most difficult 'sixty-four-dollar question' resulted in an award of that amount, if answered correctly. In time this gave rise to its use as a phrase all over the English-speaking world, meaning the most difficult or crucial question. It is much favoured by politicians, and others in authority, when confronted in interviews with a real puzzler, to which there is no easy or short answer, yet everything depends on it. A good way of beginning to talk round the question, without really answering it is to start with a smile and the statement 'That's the 64,000 dollar question', (which is an exaggeration of the original amount).

Ganged *see* PRESS ganged into it

To run the gauntlet is to risk danger, or lay oneself open to severe criticism. 'Gauntlet' comes from the Swedish *gantlope* and later *gata*, meaning a way or passage. Originally, 'to run the gauntlet' referred to a form of military punishment administered to sailors and soldiers, in which the victim was forced to run between a passageway formed by two long rows of men facing each other. Each man was armed with a rope end or stick and would deal as many harsh blows as possible.

The punishment was also used at one time in English boarding schools, when the victim was either thumped on the back with fists, or flicked, when naked, with the ends of wet towels.

To throw down the gauntlet is to issue a challenge. The gauntlet (or *le gantelet*) was a glove of jointed steel plates which was worn by knights in armour, who used it to throw down to anyone who had offended them, as a sign that they were to fight till one was slain, or confessed himself vanquished. In later years it became customary for an ordinary glove to be thrown down instead. If the challenge was accepted, the person to whom it was thrown picked it up.

To talk gibberish is derived from Geber, who was an 11th-century Arabian alchemist, and the obscure mystical jargon he wrote in to avoid the displeasure of the ecclesiastics of the day. Had he written openly this would have resulted in a severe penalty (probably death). What Geber wrote was quite unintelligible to others. Anyone who 'talks gibberish' today usually talks fast, and inarticulately, and what they are saying appears to be complete nonsense. 'Gibber' is a variant of 'jabber' which comes from the old words *Gabber* or *Gab*.

Gift horse The advice 'never to look a gift horse in the mouth' applies to other things and not just to horses. It suggests that when anything is received as a present you should not be too critical of it, or enquire too deeply as to its value. One of the ways of assessing the age of a horse is to inspect its teeth and their condition, but anyone given a horse should not inspect its teeth before accepting it as a gift, or — if they must — certainly not in front of the giver.

In the glasshouse Any serviceman who finds himself in this position is undergoing punishment by being confined to prison on a military base. The phrase takes its name from the prison at North Camp, Aldershot, which had a glass roof.

The jangling of jailers' keys, gave rise to the word, 'jankers' which was used to describe this form of punishment, although it was also used for lesser offences where the culprit was not so much imprisoned as confined to camp under close supervision for seven days or so.

There, but for the grace of God, go I This phrase was first spoken by John Bradford, in the mid-16th century, when he said: 'There, but for the grace of God, goes John Bradford', on seeing some criminals being led to execution.

The implication of the phrase, which is still in everyday use, is that none of us is perfect and that an unfortunate event, danger or disgrace which happens to someone else through their actions, or stupidity, or through chance, could just as easily have happened to us, although we have had the good luck to get away with it and avoid the consequences.

A golden handshake *see* To be BOWLER-HATTED

To play gooseberry is to act as chaperon and be present when two lovers are together, and make sure that they observe the correct codes of conduct and morals. Courting couples cannot be blamed for agreeing with the saying that 'two's company, three's a crowd', and so the unwanted third person was expected to say nothing of anything they heard or saw. They may have occasionally strolled off, in gardens or the countryside, and, presumably, sought and picked cultivated or wild gooseberries.

The gooseberry is the symbol of anticipation. When children asked where babies came from they were often told by embarrassed parents or nannies that they were found beneath a gooseberry bush. The explanation persisted into the 1920s, as did the role of chaperon.

[66]

To cut the Gordian knot

> Turn him to any cause of policy,
> The Gordian knot of it he will unloose . . .

A Gordian Knot refers to a difficult problem or task, and when Shakespeare wrote the above lines in his play *Henry V* (1.1) he was drawing on an event, which occurred over 1,900 years previously, involving Alexander the Great. When he invaded Asia Minor, Alexander came across a wagon which Gordius, the peasant-king of Phrygia, had dedicated to Jupiter, and fastened the yoke to a beam with a rope which he had knotted so ingeniously that no one could untie it. When Alexander was told that whoever undid the knot would reign over the whole empire of Asia, he wished to inspire his army and convince his enemies that he was born to conquer. So, instead of wasting time in trying to untie the knot, he solved the problem by 'cutting the Gordian Knot', with a single bold stroke of his sword.

An earlier writer, three years before Shakespeare's birth, had recorded that 'It is like the Gordian; which it is better to breake in sunder, than to labor so much in undoinge it'. The sentiment still applies today when anyone is faced with what appear to be insurmountable difficulties; the phrase serves as a reminder of the solution which can be achieved by taking decisive action, and the use of unorthodox methods.

Sour grapes is said of someone who wants something desperately but pretends not to, by saying that they don't want it, when they have failed to get it.

The saying comes to us from Aesop's fable in which a fox stood gaping under a vine, licking his lips at a most delicious cluster of grapes, and then leapt at them hundreds of times until he was exhausted, and still unable to reach them. As he went away, he covered his disappointment by saying, 'Hang 'em, they are as sour as crabs'.

Feeling groggy When this expression is used today it usually means that someone is feeling giddy, or in a shaky and unsteady state. In former times it referred to drunkenness, and got its name from the ration of rum, known as 'grog', which was issued to sailors in the Royal Navy until 1971.

In 1740, Admiral Vernon watered down the neat rum that was being issued to officers and men and earned the nickname of 'Old Grog'. This was derived from the Grogram cloak which he wore, made from a coarse fabric of silk, mohair and wool, stiffened with gum. The name stuck to the drink even when it was restored to its full strength in later years.

Be my guest During the 1950s and 60s anyone who asked if they could look at, or borrow, something of no great importance would often receive the reply, 'be my guest', which meant that they were welcome to do so. But, as had been observed over two centuries earlier 'a constant guest is never welcome'. So such requests should not be made too often if they are to receive a friendly reply.

According to Gunter *see* According to COCKER

A hair of the dog that bit you As cures for hangovers still seem to elude sufferers, one popular piece of advice is to take 'a hair of the dog that bit you'. In other words, have another drink in the morning. This refers to the ancient belief that a hair of the dog that bit one, when placed on the wound, was the best antidote to the after-effects of its bite.

To make the hair stand on end Anything which is enough 'to make the hair stand on end' indicates something frightening or horrific. There is a direct reference to this in the book of Job (4.15), 'His spirit glided past my face; the hair of my flesh stood up'. The ancient belief that fright can actually make the hair rise has a certain amount of truth in it. Hair grows in follicles (openings or depressions) to which strands of smooth muscle are attached. When the muscles contract they pull the hairs upright and make them bristle, or stand on end.

The growth of hair has always been regarded as something of a miracle, and all manner of phrases have been associated with the hair on our heads. We are told 'to keep our hair on', or keep cool and not panic in certain circumstances. If we accept the advice, and remain composed and unruffled, we do so 'without turning a hair'. A very narrow escape from a dangerous situation, on the other hand, is known as 'a hair-breadth escape', and Shakespeare mentions the phrase in *Othello*. Anyone accused of 'splitting hairs' is wasting time by arguing over trifling details. While any woman who 'lets her hair down' is 'letting herself go', or 'kicking over the traces', originating from the times when women pinned their long hair up for formal occasions, and let it down to flow freely when in private, or amongst close friends.

Halcyon days refer to happy times remembered for their peace, contentment and perfection.

Halcyon was the Greek name for the kingfisher. According to legend, Halcyone, who was the goddess of the winds, married Ceyx, King of Trachis, who drowned when his ship was wrecked in a storm at sea. Halcyone did not know of his death until it was revealed to her in a dream, whereupon she became overwhelmed with grief and threw herself into the sea, close to where his body was floating.

The gods took pity on her and reversed the tragedy by restoring Ceyx to life, and transformed both of them into kingfishers, so that they might live happily together as birds of the water. The gods also promised that whenever she and her descendants were hatching the eggs in their nests, made of fishbones floating on the ocean, that the wind would be held back and the sea remain calm.

It was said that the seven days preceding the winter solstice (the shortest day of the year in December) was the time used by these birds to build their nests on the water, and the seven days afterwards were devoted to hatching the eggs.

Although kingfishers nest in tunnels beside river banks, not on the ocean, their nests are frequently lined with fishbones, which ties in with the ancient belief, and the Mediterranean is usually calm at the time of the solstice — hence the expression 'halcyon days' denoting periods of calm and contentment.

Hammer and tongs To go at anyone, or anything, 'hammer and tongs' is to do so with great force, or to quarrel with someone very loudly. The analogy is to the work of the blacksmith who holds the hot iron with the tongs and brings the hammer down forcibly, and loudly, to beat the iron into shape. This also gives rise to other expressions such as 'hammering something home', or 'hammering an idea into someone's head'.

Close the hangar doors In the 1930s most RAF aeroplanes, and those at civilian aerodromes and flying clubs, were put inside hangars at night to protect them from possible bad weather, gales or ice. Many had no brakes, and the controls on the wings and tails could not be locked, so the precaution was not only advisable but necessary. Many of the lighter aircraft, such as de Havilland Moths, Tiger Moths, and others, had wings which could be folded so that they took up the minimum of space and, as a fee had to be paid for each day and night's use of hangar space, this innovation was welcomed by pilots and owners.

When pilots congregated in the mess, or clubhouse, at the end of the day, the talk at the bar was (and still is) invariably about flying. When this went on too long, or 'bar pilots' (those who talked a lot about flying but had little experience of it) continued to 'shoot their lines' (exaggerate their stories) they were told to 'close the hangar doors', in other words, to stop talking shop.

May as well be hanged for a sheep as a lamb — In for a penny, in for a pound Before the 1830s, when the punishments for crimes were harsh, anyone found guilty of stealing a sheep was sentenced to death by hanging. If they stole something of much less value — a lamb — the penalty was still the same. Thieves reckoned they might just as well steal a sheep as a lamb as it would provide more meat.

The phrase is similar to the more modern one of IN FOR A PENNY, IN FOR A POUND, which implies that once you have committed yourself to some undertaking, even though you may regret it, you might just as well go the whole way and make the most of the situation.

To keep harping on something is to be a bore by dwelling tediously on a subject, to talk or write endlessly on the same topic, or to keep bringing up the same point in an argument over and over again, i.e. 'to keep harping on the same string'. The phrase has been used for centuries, which is not surprising as the harp is one of the world's most ancient instruments.

It was very popular in Victorian times during musical evenings in the home when daughters were encouraged by their parents to 'delight' the guests in the drawing-room with the harp's graceful tones, as well as their own airs and graces. The drawing-room was, originally, the withdrawing room to which the ladies retired after dinner while the men continued to enjoy their wine and cigars. When the men did rejoin the ladies, they had to put up with the young ones trying to impress them with their performance, while most were unmusical, on what is one of the most difficult of all instruments to play.

[70]

Hatch *see* Eat, drink, and be MERRY, and Down the hatch

To bury the hatchet is to forget old scores and let bygones be bygones, and comes from the American Indian custom of burying their hatchets, scalp-knives, and war clubs when making peace, to show that hostilities were at an end. This is similar to the custom of shaking hands with the right hand when settling disputes or quarrels. The use of the right hand, previously the sword-hand, proved that no weapons were being carried or, if a sword was worn on some ceremonial or traditional occasion, that there was no intention of using it, and both parties wished to become friends.

To knock into a cocked hat is to act aggressively and change something out of all recognition, while to knock someone's performance into a cocked hat is to defeat them resoundingly.

The word 'knock' appears in many phrases, such as 'to knock the bottom out of an argument'; ' — one's head against a brick wall', ' — someone's head off', or ' — someone into the middle of next week'.

Cocked hats were 'tricorne' or three-cornered hats worn by gentlemen of fashion in the late 17th century. They were made by folding the round hats, which had been popular previously, into corners.

Talking through their hats This is said of those who are thought either to be insincere, or talking nonsense. If someone is accused of 'talking through his hat' this implies that what he has said is merely a form of words as he does not mean them seriously.

Three hundred years ago it was customary for men to wear their hats in church, but they would remove them and hold them in front of their mouths as they said their prayers. When these were over, they sat up and put their hats back on again.

To bury one's head in the sand is to refuse to take any notice of a difficulty or problem; to pretend that it does not exist, or think it will go away, or solve itself. The expression is based on the habit of the ostrich which is reputed to bury its head in sand when pursued and in danger, in the belief that it cannot be seen.

The ostrich, which is the largest flightless bird of Africa, up to 9 ft (2.74 m) in height, does not, in fact, do any such thing. Despite their size, and their weight of around 300 lb (136 kg), ostriches are extremely agile. When they sense the approach of predators, they bend their necks parallel to the ground to listen intently and, if in danger, they are able to

[71]

escape by running away at speeds of up to 40 mph (64 kph).

They probably give the impression that they bury their heads when they are seen bending their necks and listening close to the ground, or when attending the eggs in their nests, which consist of a simple depression scraped in the sand.

Off the top of one's head means one's first opinion, or thoughts, without having had time to consider the situation fully.

In the 1970s, it was quite common in the advertising profession for someone who had a sudden flash of inspiration and an idea for the new campaign which was under discussion to follow it up by saying, 'Let's run it up the flagpole and see who salutes it', to see what the general consensus of opinion was.

Heat *see* If you can't stand the heat, keep out of the KITCHEN

Heel taps *see* Eat, drink, and be MERRY, and No heel taps

To hobnob is to be on the closest possible friendly terms. The phrase comes from *hob* and *nob* which meant 'give and take', which was a corruption of the earlier Anglo-Saxon *hab* and *nab*, 'to have or not have'. As good friends tend to stand by and help each other out, particularly when one of their number has fallen upon less forunate times, the interpretation of the phrase becomes clear.

'To hob-nob' also applied to intimate friends drinking together, and Charles Dickens conveys something of this relationship and convivial atmosphere in *Great Expectations*:

'Have another glass!'
'With you hob and nob', returned the sergeant.
'The top of mine to the foot of yours — the foot of yours to the top of mine — Ring once, ring twice — the best tune on the Musical Glasses! Your Health'.

Hobson's choice is an expression signifying that there is only one course of action, in other words, there is no choice as there is no alternative.

The phrase had its origin in Cambridge, England, where Thomas Hobson (1544–1630) kept a large number of horses for hire in his stable. Whenever anyone wanted to hire a horse, Hobson always offered only the one nearest the stable door. Customers had to accept this and, therefore, had no choice at all.

[72]

Hobson might appear to have been unreasonable, but he was really quite the reverse as he considered his animals and used his system of 'Hobson's choice' to ensure that no horse was overworked for each one was used in strict rotation. He kept himself fit, too, because he lived to be 86 years old.

Hoist *see* Hoist with his own PETARD

Hokey-pokey implies trickery, deception or sham. It probably derives from the early 17th century when the words 'hocus-pocus' were included in conjurors' patter used to divert the attention of the audience while performing tricks.

Hokey-pokey was an early form of cheap ice-cream sold by street vendors in England.

The ice-cream drink, known as a 'sundae', came into being through a clever deception to evade a law in Virginia, USA, which made it illegal to sell soda-fountain drinks on a Sunday. An enterprising owner of a drugstore in Norfolk, Virginia, got round the problem by adding ice-cream, and crushed fruit and nuts, to the drink so that it was accepted by the authorities as food and, therefore, allowed to be sold on Sundays.

Home James, and don't spare the horses was a common command of the nobility, squires, and men about town to their private coachman to indicate that they wanted to get home as quickly as possible.

When automobiles came on the scene and took over from the horse, their engines were rated, until quite recently, in terms of horse-power. The order not to spare the horses was directed at a chauffeur.

The phrase is still called out light-heartedly to the driver by a passenger, or group of people, being offered a lift home in a private car.

By hook or by crook means to obtain something, one way or another, by fair means or foul. The phrase originated in 1100 when William Rufus, King of England, was slain by an arrow while out hunting in the New Forest, in Hampshire.

When a charcoal burner, named Purkiss, came across the king's abandoned body he took it by cart to Winchester. Although no bell was tolled nor prayer said at the arrival or burial, for the king had been a harsh man with plenty of enemies, a reward of five pieces of silver was offered to Purkiss. Instead of accepting them, he asked to be allowed to gather all the timber in the forest that he could for his trade of charcoal burning.

[73]

Strict laws forbade anyone to take any wood, except the dead branches from beneath trees, which is one reason why the New Forest is still the largest surviving medieval forest in Britain today. Purkiss, however, was granted his wish and allowed to gather all the timber he could reach by hook or by crook. In other words, all the timber that could be reached by a shepherd's crook and cut down with a billhook.

Generations of the Purkiss family have lived in the New Forest ever since, though the spelling of the name came to be changed over the centuries to 'Purkess'.

On the horns of a dilemma A dilemma, which comes from the Greek *di*, meaning twofold, and *lemma*, a thing taken or received, is a situation in which one is faced with a choice between two alternatives, either equally good or equally bad.

To be 'on the horns of a dilemma' is to be confronted with two equally distasteful alternatives and not be sure which way one should make up one's mind. The dilemma in the phrase has been likened to the horns of a bull. Whichever horn is seized, the result is likely to be equally unpleasant.

To draw in one's horns can refer to spending less of one's money, or to drawing back from a situation and refraining from action while reconsidering the matter. The phrase has been likened to the action of the snail which withdraws its horns when threatened with danger, or confronted with unfavourable circumstances.

Land snails are nocturnal as humidity is greater at night and moisture is necessary to their life. During periods of drought they will remain within their shell for weeks on end. A summer shower or wet day, however, will encourage them to venture from their hiding places. As the snail sets forth, it extends its head, then puts out two long horns which have an eye at each tip, and turn from side to side to survey all around them. The moment the snail is disturbed, or threatened, it withdraws its horns, followed by its whole body, into its shell.

(*See* 'On the horns of a dilemma'.)

To put the cart before the horse is of ancient origin and now serves as a warning against not getting our priorities right.

Obviously, the horse should come in front of the cart, but when the phrase came into being it was slightly different. Horses don't, in fact, pull carts, they *push* them, by pushing on the collar of the harness attached to the cart. So the original phrase was 'Don't *push* the cart before the horse'.

[74]

Horse *see* GIFT horse

To get off one's hobby horse (or soapbox) Originally, a hobby horse was a type of velocipede, first used in England in the mid-1600s, on which the rider sat and pushed himself along with his feet. Although primitive, presumably the experience was enjoyable for the word 'hobby', apart from its archaic reference to a 'small horse', came to mean one's favourite subject or pastime. Within a few years, it was said that 'almost every person hath some hobby horse or other wherein he prides himself'. (In other words, some pet theory or subject on which they dwelt tediously.)

There is an old saying that 'a hobby may be ridden to death' and if the advice of the 18th-century novelist and humorist, Laurence Sterne, had been heeded, in the metaphorical sense, many unwilling listeners would have been saved untold hours of boredom. For, 'so long', he wrote, 'as a man rides his hobby horse peaceably and quietly along the King's highway, and neither compels you or me to get up behind him, — pray, Sir, what have either you or I to do with it?'

Nowadays, to be told to get off one's hobby horse — or soapbox (on which speakers stand in public places to air their opinions loudly) — is to imply that they are overdoing their pet subject, becoming boring, or that what they are saying has all been heard before.

Horses *see* Don't CHANGE horses in mid-stream

Horses for courses When someone uses this phrase in general conversation, they are usually implying that it would be better if people stuck to the thing they know, or do, best. In the racing game, it is used to suggest that some horses run on certain courses better than on others — appreciating a left-hand circuit, perhaps, rather than a right-hand one, or vice-versa.

Any horse that is shortsighted would be unlikely to do well on any course, one would imagine. However, in the Racing Museum at York racecourse there is a pair of spectacles, with bifocal lenses, prescribed by a Yorkshire vet for a short-sighted trotting horse.

So far as spectators are concerned, one of the most popular, and certainly the most beautiful, courses is that of 'glorious Goodwood', set amidst the green undulating country of the Sussex Downs, which Edward VII described as 'a garden with racing tacked on'.

[75]

To eat humble pie means to be prepared to suffer humiliation by admitting that one is wrong, whether one believes this to be so or not, and to apologize for what one has done or said.

The expression probably arose from medieval dining customs. After hunting deer, and other animals, the choicest meat was served to the master of the household, his family and guests, while the heart, liver and kidneys — known as 'umbles' and considered less desirable — were given to the staff, baked in the form of pies. During the course of time, 'umble' became confused with 'humble'.

The tip of the iceberg If something is referred to as 'only the tip of the iceberg' this should be taken as a warning for it indicates that one is faced with only a small part of a far greater problem or difficulty.

The word *Berg* means mountain. Icebergs (or ice mountains) break off from glaciers floating in the sea. An iceberg measuring 100 ft (30 m) above the sea may be as much as 700 ft (213 m) beneath the surface, which obviously constitutes a serious hazard to shipping. Icebergs in the Atlantic are much larger; one sighted in the South Pacific Ocean in 1956 was found to be 208 miles (335 km) long and 60 miles (96 km) wide. Sometimes they exceed 500 ft (152 m) above the water, with as much as nine times this size hidden below the surface.

As such large areas of icebergs are submerged a ship can strike the unseen part while still some distance away from the part which is visible. One of the greatest marine disasters in peace-time occurred at night in 1912 when the giant steamship *Titanic* struck the under-water shelf of an iceberg, on her maiden voyage from Liverpool to New York. She sank in less than two hours with the loss of all but 706 of her 2,300 passengers and crew.

When icebergs are observed from a safe distance they tend to overwhelm with the beauty of their fantastic shapes, varying colours and glints of light. Even at night, they glow with a peculiar whiteness, known as 'ice blink', caused by the reflection of scattered rays of light from the sky on the ice.

The warning in the phrase 'the tip of the iceberg' requires all the more attention, therefore, because all is not what it seems, and the danger, or problem, we are confronted with may be far greater than we think.

To go Indian file is when a number of people walk in a single line. The phrase arose from the tactics of the American Indians in which each warrior stepped in the footprints of the man ahead, and the last man obliterated the line of footprints, so that no one should know that a large number of warriors had passed that way.

To add insult to injury is to make things worse or wound someone, unjustly, by what one says or does when they have already suffered enough.

The phrase has been in continuous use in everyday speech for centuries, which is not surprising as it arose from one of the fables of classical times quoted by the Latin writer Phaedrus, based on an early version of Aesop. A bald man, attempting to kill a fly which had bitten him on the head, missed the insect and gave himself a sound smack, whereupon the fly said, 'You wanted to kill me for a mere touch. What will you do to yourself, now that you have added insult to injury?'

Not one iota, jot or tittle means the smallest possible degree or amount. When the phrase is used in its most popular sense it indicates that the speaker either does not care, or does not propose to give anything at all.

The 'iota' (or 'i') is the smallest letter in the Greek alphabet, alternatively known as 'jot'. The 'tittle' is the dot over the 'i', with all three words meaning a tiny amount.

The 'yod', which is the smallest letter in the Hebrew alphabet, translates as 'jot' and in Matthew 5: 18 we read '. . . one jot or one tittle shall in no wise pass from the law, till all be fulfilled'.

To strike while the iron is hot is to take advantage of a situation, or act at the right time. This saying, which goes back to the 14th century, comes from the blacksmith who must strike the metal of a horseshoe when it is red hot, and at exactly the right temperature, to create the precise shape and fit required.

[77]

Too many irons in the fire is a warning not to have too many jobs or activities on the go at the same time. The phrase refers to the blacksmith's forge, where if the smith had too many irons heating in the fire at the same time he couldn't do his job properly, as he was unable to use them all before some had cooled off.

To dot the I's and cross the T's is to pay the greatest attention to detail when carrying out a job, particularly in preparing and checking documents, agreements, or contracts, in which the utmost importance is attached to every word contained in them. The phrase originated when official documents were hand written and confusion could obviously arise if these two letters of the alphabet were not completed by the clerk.

Part of the phrase came to be adapted by the navy in the form of 'Go back and cross the T's . . .' which would be directed at a helmsman who had steered an erratic course and 'written their name' in the ship's wake.

Kilroy was here This phrase came into being during World War II when it was written on walls wherever the American Forces had been. It still appears in Britain to this day. Its origin is not certain, though it is said that a shipyard inspector in Massachusetts chalked the words on equipment he had inspected, in much the same way as chalk marks are used to indicate cases cleared through customs.

If you can't stand the heat, keep out of the kitchen This phrase was originated by the President of the USA, Harry S. Truman, and used frequently by him during the early 1950s. It was taken up in Britain some twenty years later, and used widely in everyday speech to imply that if anyone could not stand the pace, or strain, they should not get involved or take part in whatever was being undertaken or proposed.

[78]

Knock *see* Knock into a cocked HAT

Rate of knots Anyone who does anything at the 'rate of knots' is doing it extremely swiftly. Originally, it was a nautical phrase referring to divisions marked by knots tied on the log-line, which was used as a measurement of speed, in which the number of knots run out in the ship's wake were counted and timed with a sand glass. If a ship is making 20 knots, it is travelling at 20 nautical miles per hour. A knot, or nautical mile, is 6,080 feet or 1.8532 km.

To know the ropes — Know one's onions TO KNOW THE ROPES was an expression coined in the days of sailing ships when a knowledge of all the intricacies of the ship's rigging was vital. Sailors needed to know every rope, and how it should be handled and used. The phrase subsequently came into use during the 19th century to refer to anyone who knew exactly how to handle something. Such a person was regarded as an expert in their craft or profession.

A similar phrase, 'to know all the answers', implies resourcefulness and intelligence, but there are always those who *think* they know all the answers when, in fact, they know little or nothing about a subject. It has been observed that anyone who claims to know all the answers can only do so because they have failed to understand all the questions.

TO KNOW ONE'S ONIONS applies to anyone who is experienced and really knows his subject, or who has a profound knowledge of things in general. Obviously they are clever, but it is often possible to join their ranks if the advice of Dr Samuel Johnson (1709–1784) is heeded: 'Knowledge is of two kinds. We know a subject ourselves, or we know where we can find information on it'.

If the search for knowledge 'turns our head', or sends one off one's onion' (head) this phrase means that one has become deranged, over-excited, mentally exhausted, or irrational.

On the other hand, anyone who succeeds in acquiring great knowledge, while remaining sane, must always guard against their success in 'going to their head' and remain humble. Otherwise they might run the risk of being ridiculed and 'cut down to size'. The lines of the Norwegian dramatist Henrik Ibsen's in *Peer Gynt* serve as a warning:

> You're not an emperor, you're an onion!
> Now my dear Peer, I'm going to peel you,
> However little you may enjoy it.

To knuckle under is to give in or acknowledge defeat. Nowadays, we associate the knuckle with a finger-joint, but in former times it also referred to other joints, such as the knee-joint. 'To knuckle under' was therefore equivalent to kneeling, which signified submission.

Fighters always clench their fists with their knuckles uppermost, whether wearing gloves or not. Hands held out with the knuckles downwards indicate that there is no threat, or malicious intent.

The phrase is similar to that of 'to knock under', from the 17th-century rhyme, 'He that flinches his glass and to drink is not able; Let him quarrel no more, but knock under the table', which, in this case, referred to succumbing in a drinking bout. At other times, to knock the under side of the table with the knuckle served as an acknowledgement of defeat in an argument.

Lamb *see* May as well be HANGED for a sheep as a lamb

Rest on one's laurels — Look to one's laurels The laurel has for long been the emblem of victory, and of poets who have achieved recognition for the excellence of their works. The heads of Homer and Virgil, Plutarch and Tasso are all represented crowned with laurel. The 'evergreen' is chosen to signify that they will be remembered for all time, hence the term 'poet laureate', introduced during the late 17th century, when John Dryden became the first to receive the official title.

Laurel was not only used to crown victors, heroes, and those who had achieved distinction. Many, who aspired to such heights, placed laurel leaves under their pillows to acquire strength for victory, or inspiration for their poetry.

Today, anyone who is said to be 'resting on their laurels' is content with the success they have already achieved, having reached the stage where they no longer want to strive for further glory. Whereas, to 'look to one's laurels' is a warning to continue maximum effort, maintain one's position, and not underestimate the competition or task ahead.

Lead *see* Lead in your PENCIL

Swinging the lead — Plumbing the depths It used to be common for the depth of water beneath a boat to be checked by a length of line, with a lead weight at the end, marked at intervals in a distinctive way. Although the method was, and still is, used all over the world, 'lead-swinging' tends to be associated with the old-time Mississippi river steamboats. As the lookout threw the lead-line in the water and called out the readings to the pilot he would say 'mark one' for one fathom, and 'mark twain' (mark two fathoms) using the old-fashioned word for 'two', as he took the soundings. It is from this that the American humorist and novelist, Samuel Langhorne Clemens, (1835–1910) took his pen-name, 'Mark Twain'. He became celebrated not only in America but all over Europe, and beyond. Mark Twain was at one time a river pilot himself, and among his major works was *Life on the Mississippi*.

Nowadays, the depth of water can be known instantly at the touch of a switch through the use of electronic echo-sounders. In the old lead-swinging days, however, the job looked leisurely and easy, and it is from this appearance, rather than fact, that the phrase SWINGING THE LEAD probably arose. It describes anyone who is malingering, trying to avoid work or not putting their heart in a job, or maybe shamming illness. It was said that some of the lookouts called out fictitious soundings instead of the correct depths. No doubt they knew the waters well and erred on the safe side otherwise they would have been called upon to work hard to free the boat if it became grounded.

The other phrase to PLUMB THE DEPTHS also came into being from the swinging of a piece of lead on a string (plumb) into the water to discover its depth, and is used in its general sense to refer to the state where a person, or group of people, have gone way past 'mark twain' (or two fathoms) and sunk to the lowest levels of misfortune and unhappiness.

To turn over a new leaf The early Egyptians found that they could make a material for writing on from the leaves of the giant water-reed *papyrus*, from which we get the word 'paper'. Each single thickness of paper in a book, or manuscript (i.e. its top and reverse side) is still called a 'folio' from the Latin *folium*, meaning a leaf.

Another Latin word, *sceda*, was used for the papyrus-strip which made up the Egyptian overseer's ledger, in which the amount of work carried out by each person under his control was recorded, hence the origin of the word 'schedule'. If work falls behind schedule, 'to turn over a new leaf' (to a clean page) indicates a fresh start, or a chance to mend one's ways and improve on one's past record.

To take French leave is to leave one's work, without giving notice or obtaining permission, or slipping away from a social occasion without saying goodbye to the host or hostess. It can also mean taking something without permission. The practice is attributed to the French by the English, and to the English by the French.

A curtain lecture

> Now stir the fire, and close the shutters fast,
> Let fall the curtains, wheel the sofa round,
> And, while the bubbling and loud-hissing urn,
> Throws up a steamy column, and the cups,
> That cheer but not inebriate, wait on each,
> So let us welcome peaceful evening in.

> *William Cowper*

That peaceful evening scene, described by the 18th-century poet, paints an idyllic picture. Curtains were not only used at windows in former times, but hung around beds where, all too often, the scene was anything but peaceful. For, after they had been closed, the private scoldings given by wives to husbands were frequent enough to give birth to what came to be known as 'a curtain lecture'.

The phrase is still used today to denote a reproof or ticking-off given in secret, behind closed doors, in some secluded place out of earshot of others.

Show a leg was originally a naval phrase, short for 'show a leg there or a purser's stocking', from the days when women were allowed on board HM ships. When the ratings were called out in the morning, they had to jump to it. Any women in the beds or hammocks had, literally, to show a bare leg or stocking over the side to show that they were the occupants, and they were allowed a 'lie-in'.

Officers were jealous of their ship's reputation, and they made sure that only smart and attractive women were allowed on board. Those who didn't come up to the high standard required were sent back to shore. Sometimes women were permitted to accompany the men on a voyage and, despite the 'screening' process, there were many 'loose' women who managed to remain aboard whose sole interest was in exchanging sex for money.

Lemon *see* The ANSWER's a lemon

A lick and a promise is descriptive of a job of work, used particularly when something has been cleaned in a quick and superficial way, just as a cat gives a quick lick to its paw, before passing it briefly over its face without giving it a good wash, even though it may do so more thoroughly later.

To lick into shape When hunters in times past saw mother bears licking what appeared to be the shapeless mass of their newly-born cubs they assumed that she was, literally, shaping them with her tongue. Bear cubs weigh almost nothing, and are ridiculously small compared with their parents so it would have been difficult to see what the mother bear was really doing, unless studied at extremely close quarters. Although subsequent generations know that she was not shaping, but cleaning them, the phrase which is of 15th-century origin, is still widely used when anyone is making anything, or anybody, more presentable.

Lightning *see* Lightning STRIKE

To gild the lily is to attempt, foolishly, to try and improve on something which is already perfect. Shakespeare, who mentions the lily in his works on more than two dozen occasions, wrote: 'To gild refined gold, to paint the lily . . . is wasteful and ridiculous excess.' The white lily, which is the emblem of majesty and purity, is one of the oldest and most beautiful flowers in existence and, therefore, without need of any further addition of superfluous ornament.

In the limelight Limelight, which is also known as Drummond light after Thomas Drummond who invented it in 1826, is an intense white light obtained by heating a cylinder of lime in an oxy-hydrogen flame. It was used originally in a lighthouse to assist shipping off the Kentish coast. Subsequently, it was developed to obtain special lighting effects in the theatre, mainly, by directing its powerful beam on to one actor at a time to highlight their performance, in the same way as spotlights are used today. To be 'in the limelight' is a popular phrase to describe anyone who is in the full glare of publicity and public interest.

[83]

Lining the pocket Used in its figurative sense this expression came into being in Regency times when it referred to the giving of money to further one's cause. At this time the English Dandy, 'Beau' Brummell, friend of the Prince Regent (who became George IV), dictated fashion, though neither rich nor born of high-estate.

Rivalry amongst tailors for Beau Brummel's patronage was intense. One would imagine that the Court tailor would be sure of obtaining this, but to make certain he made Beau Brummell a present of a dress-coat lined with banknotes. His precaution paid off, for Brummell wrote to thank him, stating that he liked the coat — and especially the lining.

Lock, stock and barrel refers to the three principal parts of old guns, and is used to indicate totality — the whole thing. Although it is a very old expression, it is still used frequently. If one were turning out some goods from an old attic, which were no longer required, for instance, someone might offer to buy or take them off you 'lock, stock and barrel', meaning that they are prepared to take the lot.

Lotus eaters are people whose only interest centres around a life of idleness, carefree luxury and comfort. The phrase was derived from Homer's *Odyssey*.

When unfavourable winds drove the ships of Odysseus off course on their way home from war against the Trojans and, eventually, land was sighted he sent a party ashore to obtain water. As they set foot on what turned out to be an enchanting land, inhabited by friendly people, they were given the fruit of the lotus-tree to eat. The fruit was like no other fruit and its effect was to make all who eat it forget about their friends and homes and lose all desire of returning to their ships or native country. Their only wish was to live in lotus-land for ever in an idle, dreamy state of ease and luxury.

Their dream was short-lived, however, for when Odysseus learned of the influence of the lotus-tree which had put them under the spell of forgetfulness, he went ashore with others of his crew, bound the dreamy sailors hand and foot, and carried them back to their ships. He set sail away from the land of the Lotus-eaters as fast as he could.

Tennyson's poem *The Lotos-Eaters* gives a vivid description of the sailors' feelings when they set foot on Lotus-land and longed to stay there forever and 'no longer roam'.

Lumbered with it At one time many houses contained a lumber-room in which disused articles of furniture were placed, together with a wide assortment of broken, useless, and cumbersome items which were taking up valuable space elsewhere.

Nowadays, with smaller houses, many people still hate to part with things. Although they don't want certain articles today, they might want them one day, so they hang on to them and put the 'lumber' in the attic.

On the other hand, there are always those who hold to the belief of 'good riddance to bad rubbish' who cannot bear to hoard old items, so they offer them to others. Often, for the sake of maintaining friendships or good relationships, it is difficult to refuse such 'gifts', and so one becomes 'lumbered' with them. The phrase also applies to an unwanted job or duty which is impossible to decline, or get out of.

Lute *see* The RIFT within the lute

Mad as a hatter (or March hare) is descriptive of someone who acts in an odd or seemingly stupid way. It is possible that the original mad hatter was an eccentric who lived in Buckinghamshire, England, during the 17th century, who gave away all his goods to the poor and lived on the leaves of weeds and grass. The phrase was used in America some thirty years before Lewis Carroll wrote about the Mad Hatter's tea party in *Alice in Wonderland*, and was based on the old belief that the people who made felt hats went mad as a result of the mercury (or mercurous nitrate) used during the process.

Among the more severe effects produced was the nervous affliction of chorea, known as St Vitus's Dance. At one time it was believed that anyone who danced on the feast day of the Christian martyr would be ensured of good health for the year. This wild dancing, which was accompanied by great leaps, for hours on end, became a mania in Europe until the nervous plague ceased to frighten them.

The phrase as 'mad as a March hare', which also appears in *Alice in Wonderland*, is also used to describe anyone behaving in an odd, or apparently foolish way. Hares tend to be unusually wild in March, during their main breeding season. Their antics, leaping, boxing, and chasing across the countryside during their courtship displays, make it appear to observers as if they are completely mad.

Your Majesty Henry VIII was the first English monarch to be addressed with this term, although it was not used regularly until Stuart times. Henry IV was known as 'His Grace', Henry VI as 'His Excellent Grace', Edward IV as 'High and Mighty Prince', while Henry VIII had been known previously as 'His Highness' while he was a young king.

Another change, in custom rather than title, came about in the first half of the 19th century, during the reign of William IV, close friend of Admiral Lord Nelson, known popularly as 'Sailor Billy', who served happily in the Royal Navy for eleven years, starting as an able seaman. It is the custom to stand up when the loyal toast to His or Her Majesty's health is drunk. When the 'sailor king' rose to his feet to acknowledge the toast, however, he hit his head on a beam in the wardroom. As a result it has been the Royal Navy's privilege to remain seated since then.

One of the Navy's popular toasts is 'Sweethearts and wives' . . . often followed by 'and may they never meet'. Or, in different mood . . . 'may our sweethearts become our wives, and our wives remain our sweethearts'.

Man *see* A man of STRAW

To steal a march on someone is to anticipate their actions and gain a secret advantage over them. The 'march' in this phrase originally referred to the distance covered by troops in a day. As the time of arrival could be calculated quite easily, armies sometimes moved by night or 'stole a march' so as they could spring a surprise on the enemy.

Up to the mark Anything that is not 'up to the mark' is considered not up to standard. The 'mark' in the phrase refers to the 'hall-mark' stamped by the assay office on gold and silver articles which are of approved quality.

Originally, when wine was tasted before being served to monarchs and people of importance to make certain it was not poisoned, the person ordered to do this was instructed 'to take the assay' (to test or try it). While the term 'hall-mark' came into being from the assaying, testing, and stamping done at the Goldsmiths' Hall. In a more general sense, anyone who is 'up to the mark' feels fit, confident, and is in excellent form and considered, by others, as first rate.

Betty Martin *see* ALL my eye

The real McCoy is a phrase which originated in Scotland just over one hundred years ago as 'the real Mackay', and referred to people and things of the highest quality and, in particular, to a brand of whisky.

Later, in America, it became 'the real McCoy', in honour of an outstanding boxer of that name, who is said to have done everything he could to avoid being provoked by a drunk who insisted on quarrelling with him. Despite warnings from all present, the drunk started fighting McCoy who, finally, knocked him out to put an end to things. On regaining consciousness the drunk got up, dusted himself down, and said: 'You're right, it is the real McCoy.' The phrase is still used today to denote 'the real thing'.

The best laid schemes of mice and men

> The best laid schemes o' mice an' men
> Gang aft a-gley.

Robert Burns' poem *To a Mouse* warns us that no matter how carefully things are planned they can, and often do, go wrong, with the result:

> An' lea'e us nought but grief an' pain
> For promis'd joy.

The only precaution we can take is that when we think that we have planned something right, we need to check, and check again, to make sure that it *is* right, to lessen the chances of failure, disappointment, or even disaster.

Eat, drink, and be merry — Bottoms up — Down the hatch — Bumpers all round, and no heel taps — Beer money — Having a ball This phrase comes from the Bible where, in Ecclesiastes 8: 15, we read: 'A man hath no better thing under the sun, than to eat, and to drink, and to be merry.' There is a further reference in Isaiah 22: 13, 'Let us eat and drink; for tomorrow we shall die.'

That one should enjoy oneself now, while one can, is a lesson which man seems to have been particularly good at learning. The only drink available to the first men, however, was that which came to be known as

'Adam's ale', meaning water. Since then, every type of wine, ale and alcohol has been produced, and one of the great excuses for consuming it is to drink someone's health, with such phrases as BOTTOMS UP, DOWN THE HATCH and many more.

The Anglo-Saxons were great eaters, and their favourite drink was mead which was made from honey. When Edward the Martyr became Saxon King of England in 975 AD he was only thirteen years old. His stepmother wanted her own son Ethelred, who was ten years old, to be king. She had failed but, three years later, arranged with a servant to have Edward stabbed to death at Corfe Castle while drinking a horn of wine. Edward's half-brother, Ethelred, nicknamed 'Ethelred the Un-ready', was weak and self-indulgent, though it must be said in his favour that during his thirty-eight year reign he fought bravely when necessary, and he had more than his fair share of bad luck.

Although Edward's murder, while drinking a horn of wine, happened a long time ago, many of the pewter tankards introduced later had glass bottoms so that their owners, while drinking, could see any enemy approaching. The expression 'bottoms up' is used as a toast today when drinking with others.

'Bumper' is a term usually applied to good harvests, but in ancient times the Romans drank the health of a mistress by drinking a bumper (or full glass of wine) to each letter of her name. This, too, came to be adapted to modern times and the person buying drinks for friends in an inn called out BUMPERS ALL ROUND, AND NO HEEL-TAPS. This meant that everyone was to have another drink, whether they wanted it or not, and that the bumpers (glasses or tankards) were to be drunk in full. Anyone discovered pouring their drink in the aspidistra, or other convenient pot plant, or who left some of the drink in his glass, was branded as a 'heel-tapper'.

The word 'wassail' (which means 'be whole, be well') was often used as a toast in times past. It also referred to drinking bouts and festive occasions. No new year's eve was complete without the wassail bowl, containing wines and fruit, or spiced ale.

Hops seen floating in a cool, clear, glass-tankard of beer used to be one of the delights of country folk. They would hold it up to the light, often for thirty seconds or more, before drinking it. Quality was important, and if they did not like the beer at one inn they chose to drink at another. In Saxon times quality counted even more: the city of Chester had a severe law against those who brewed bad ale. They were either placed in a ducking chair, and plunged into a pool of muddy water, or made to pay a forfeit of four shillings.

Beer was not made with hops in Saxon times and it was the beginning of the 14th century before they were first used in the breweries of the Netherlands. They were not introduced into England until nearly two centuries later.

Beer is a very ancient drink; even the Egyptians made a liquor they called barley wine. By the beginning of the 18th century in England, there were three main types of beer available: ale (a strong malt liquor); 'twopenny' (an inferior kind of beer which sold at that price per pint); and ordinary beer. People often asked for mixtures (such as half and half, just as today when we require 'mild and bitter'). In 1730, a brewer named Harwood invented a liquor (known as 'entire') which united all three flavours of ale, beer and twopenny into one cask. It was a strengthening drink and so much favoured by porters, and other working people, that it eventually came to be called 'porter'.

In the early 1800s, the beer issued to British soldiers was stopped for over twenty years and replaced by the issue of an allowance of one penny a day. This is how the phrase BEER MONEY came into being, to describe spending money used for alcohol and pleasure. Sailors were more fortunate with their issue of grog (rum) . . . (see 'feeling groggy'). When the hands had finished the most difficult and dangerous job of 'splicing the mainbrace' they received twice the normal, a double tot of rum, and the phrase was taken up generally as an excuse to celebrate almost anything, or any occasion. 'Down the hatch' was originally a Naval phrase, before being taken up by civilians, which arose through the comparison of the mouth to an open hatch, leading to the lower parts of the ship below deck.

One popular innovation introduced into English homes in the 1730s, consisted of circular trays, of varying size, spaced at intervals one above the other, on a central stem and base which ran on castors. The trays were designed to contain wine, spirits, and glasses. The device, known as a 'dumb-waiter' ensured that as no servants needed to be present, no confidences would be overheard.

When it comes to food (in the 'eat, drink, and be merry' phrase) it seems strange that anyone should have 'died for want of a lobster', but this is precisely what happened at a feast arranged for Louis XIV. When the chef was informed that the lobsters required for the sauce had not arrived, he considered it such a disgrace to his personal prestige, and his craft, that he went straight to his room and thrust a sword through his body.

The nobility in England had been eating with gargantuan appetites for centuries. (The word gargantuan, which means enormous, comes from

Gargantua, the giant hero of proverbial appetite, in the satire of that name by the celebrated French humorist, Francois Rabelais.)

When the Earl of Warwick gave an entertainment in the reign of Henry VI, it lasted several days, and 3,500 persons were present. The provisions consisted of 300 quarters of wheat, 80 oxen, upwards of 1,000 sheep, and other things in similar profusion. The Tudors ate large quantities of food at meals, which consisted of many courses, although breakfast was quite a modest affair, in which bread was eaten, and washed down with a mug of beer. This was followed by dinner, anytime between 11 and 12 o'clock in the morning, with supper being the main meal, and taking the form of a banquet in the large houses, in which the eating frequently continued for three hours or more. When Henry VIII came to the throne he was young, handsome, well educated, an excellent dancer and fine musician, with a great zest for life, feasting and merrymaking. He tends to be remembered not only for his rumbustious behaviour and feasting, but as a cruel, fat man who married six times.

Breakfast became more substantial during Stuart times and included cold meat. Mid-day dinner lasted longer than before, and the main meal of supper started at five or six o'clock in the evening, followed by singing, dancing, and merrymaking, by which time most people were drunk.

During the early 18th century, breakfast parties held around ten a.m. became popular among fashionable people. Working people breakfasted modestly at the same time, after having risen early and laboured for some four hours or so. The last meal of the day was still known as supper, and the humble folk had it at eight o'clock, or thereabouts, after a long and hard day's work. The wealthy waited until the small hours after a dance or party (having eaten well at dinner during the afternoon).

The word 'dance' was not used by élite society. When they gave a dance it was a 'ball', being the French *bal*, from the Latin *ballare*, to dance. From this we get the modern phrase of HAVING A BALL (i.e. a good time).

Grist to the mill — To go through the mill — Run of the mill Any grist (corn) which was brought to the old watermills and windmills for grinding was good for business, for without it the mills would have remained idle. The full phrase 'all's grist that comes to the mill' meant that everything brought to the mill would be made use of and not be wasted. It is still used to this day as another way of expressing thanks for a gift, or offer of help to further a cause, and implies that all contributions and offers of assistance, large or small, are welcome.

Watermills were used by the Greeks during the 1st century BC, while the oldest known windmills used for grinding corn were those in Persia

(Iran) in the 7th century AD. The Domesday Book records 5,264 watermills in use in Britain between 1080 and 1086 AD.

Windmills first appeared in England during the 12th century and at one time there were 10,000 of them. A gradual decline began at the beginning of the 19th century, and the numbers had dwindled to around 300 by the 1930s. The relics of many can still be seen in the countryside today, though there are probably less than a couple of dozen still working.

The grinding machinery was massive, intricate, and heavy and gave rise to the expression TO GO THROUGH THE MILL, meaning to have a hard time ('to go through it'), or to learn anything thoroughly by undergoing training and gaining long experience.

RUN OF THE MILL, on the other hand, refers to anything which is average or ordinary, or taken as a matter of course.

Hot from the mint is an expression used to describe anything 'brand new' which has, literally, just been made; or any piece of confidential information which is being told for the first time and is, thus, likely to become a fresh source of gossip. Originally, it referred to the mint where money is coined.

At one time, there was a mint in almost every county, until these were abolished by law in 1695, during the reign of William III, and the authority to coin money could only be exercised by one national mint, housed first in the Tower of London, then in a building erected, in 1810, on Tower Hill, known today as the Royal Mint.

Each year on Mayoring (or mayor-making') Day at the ancient Cinque Port of Rye, in Sussex, a custom is still carried out to maintain its historic link with the past. For, as the clock strikes noon, it has long been the tradition for the mayor, on taking office, to scatter shovelfuls of heated coins from the balcony of an upper storey, while crowds of children scrapped and scrambled for them below.

Originally, the coins were 'hot from the mint' and consisted of coppers, though an occasional half-sovereign or two, extra hot, were scattered amonst them. Nowadays, they are pennies only, and the custom was continued to remind the citizens that, in its heyday, the town was regarded of sufficient importance to possess its own mint and issue its own coins.

The last of the Mohicans referred to the last of the tribe, but later came to be adapted to mean the last of anything. The phrase originated, during the early 19th century, from the novel of that title by the American author, James Fenimore Cooper, who became famous for his vivid tales of the Indians, as well as his sea stories. His family founded the village of Cooperstown, in the shores of Ostego Lake, now part of New York State. It was here that he spent his early years in daily contact with the Indians, which gave him the background material he needed to write of the pioneer life.

Black Monday As Monday is the day on which a return to work has to be made after the weekend break, and it also marks the official start of a new term at school, it has never been a popular day. Those Mondays during which everything seems to go wrong that could go wrong have come to be known as 'black Mondays'.

The description originated over six hundred years ago when it was applied to a storm which was so hideous, according to the *Chronicles* of Holinshed (or Hollingshead), that it 'seemed the world should have ended'. The storm first occurred during Edward III's campaign in France in the year 1360, on a foul black day of wind and hail, so cold that many died on horseback. It was followed a fortnight later by another storm of hail, lightning and thunder, which resulted in more knights in armour being struck by lightning and killed than had fallen in the previous battles of Crécy and Poitiers. Some chroniclers say that it was this storm which prompted Edward III to give up his claim to the French throne, make peace, and accept possession of the large province of Aquitaine in compensation.

Monday's child One of the first things many people do when they buy a newspaper or magazine is to turn to the horoscope page to see what the stars have to say in foretelling their future. In the Middle Ages, it was common for an astrologer to be present at births so that observation of the sky and planets could be made at the precise time and date of a child's birth. Only the wealthy could afford the luxury of such accurate predictions, and the less well-off had to make do with rhymes such as this one compiled by A. E. Bray from *Traditions of Devonshire*, 1838:

> Monday's child is fair of face,
> Tuesday's child is full of grace,
> Wednesday's child is full of woe,
> Thursday's child has far to go,
> Friday's child is loving and giving,
> Saturday's child works hard for a living,
> And the child that is born on the Sabbath day,
> Is bonny and blithe, and good and gay.

[92]

Beer money *see* Eat, drink, and be MERRY and No heel taps.

Pin money Before pins were invented in France in 1543, ladies used small skewers made of wood, bone, and ivory. Catherine Howard, Henry VIII's fifth wife, was the first queen to make use of pins in England. They were considered a great luxury, and not fit for common use. Makers were not allowed to sell them in an open shop, except on two days of the year at the beginning of January. This gave rise to the old custom of husbands giving their wives money at the beginning of the year to buy a few pins, and explains how money allowed to a wife for her own private spending came to be called 'pin money'.

Money doesn't grow on trees Numerous phrases, proverbs, and quotations have been written about money since it was first introduced in ancient times to replace the bartering of goods and possessions. Some of them imply that money is not important but those who hold this view usually have plenty of it, whereas those who disagree do not! There are others who consider that 'money is the root of all evil'. However, this is a misquotation for, as we read in The First Epistle of Paul to Timothy (6: 10), it is not money itself but 'the *love* of money (that) is the root of all evil'. Scholars interpret this further by adding 'but not the only root'.

Without an alternative to money we have to live with it. Although money is not everything, having some helps. In fact, if we are honest, few would disagree with the sentiments of Arthur Hugh Clough, the 19th-century English poet who made many pertinent observations about life, including:

> How pleasant it is to have money, heigh-ho!
> How pleasant it is to have money.

Acquiring money is seldom easy, neither is the proper management of it. The phrase 'money doesn't grow on trees' serves as a reminder to those who imagine otherwise, for whatever they may think, money is not always plentiful, available, nor readily obtained.

The earliest known coins, which were made of gold and silver, are those of the Lydians in Asia Minor (now Turkey), which date from the 7th century BC. Undated coins had existed in the previous century and a phrase from those ancient times 'As rich as Croesus', a famous king of Lydia, came into being because he was judged to be the wealthiest of all monarchs.

The word 'money' has the same origin as 'mint' and comes from the Latin *moneta*, which is derived from the Temple of Juno Moneta, the goddess, in whose temple at Rome money was coined. The bronze *as* was the earliest Roman coin, introduced shortly after 300 BC. Two silver coins the *sestertius*, and the *denarius*, worth respectively four and sixteen times the *as*, followed. Julius Caesar was the first reigning ruler to have his head depicted on coins, thereby starting the tradition followed through the centuries in other countries throughout the world.

Before long, the clipping and filing off of small particles from gold and silver coins became profitable, and a great attraction for dishonest people. To prevent this, the gold and silver coins were subsequently made with raised and milled edges which would show clearly if they had been tampered with.

The first *pening*, the penny, used by the Anglo-Saxons was originally made of silver. It was not until 1797 that the penny was made of copper, with bronze coins replacing copper ones in England in 1860. Before decimalization in Britain it was still common for beggars and those down on their luck to use the original term in 'Spare a copper, Guv'nor', hoping for several coppers to buy a cup of tea and something to eat. The American phrase is similar, 'Brother, can you spare a dime?'

Tea, and tobacco, were themselves used as money at different times in many countries. The tea-money consisted of bricks made up from small broken tea leaves and dust, which was pressed into hard compact blocks. Many primitive peoples used shells for money, hence the more modern Western expression of 'I'll take every conch (or cowrie) shell you've got', meaning 'I want all your money, so that you can pay me in full'.

There are no lack of proverbs about the management of money. From the 16th century there is, 'A fool and his money are soon parted', which is self-explanatory; or, on a prudent note, 'never spend your money before you have it.' From the 17th century there is 'lend your money and lose your friend'; and a century later the warning not to 'throw good money after bad', and to 'take care of the pence and the pounds will take care of themselves'.

The general summing up should be left to Charles Dickens in *David Copperfield*. His immortal character Mr Micawber says: 'Annual income twenty pounds, annual expenditure nineteen (pounds) nineteen (and) six, result happiness. Annual income twenty pounds, annual expenditure twenty pounds ought and six, result misery'.

There will always be those who throw caution to the winds and are reckless with money, and who follow the 17th century advice, 'in for a penny, in for a pound' and who, having lost money, will throw in more. In its more general sense, this phrase implies that once something has been begun, there can be no turning back, and it must be concluded at all costs, whatever the obstacles or difficulties may turn out to be.

There is one form of money, however, which certainly doesn't grow on trees and requires no advice as to its use as it is always greatly cherished by those who receive it — 'Maundy Money'. On Maundy Thursday, the day before Good Friday, it was once the custom for the reigning British monarch to wash the feet of the chosen poor, as a token of humility in memory of Christ washing his disciples' feet at the Last Supper. Edward II did so in the early 14th century. When Edward III came to the throne, in 1327, he introduced the practice of distributing *maunds*, or doles, in the form of food and clothing to the needy. The feet-washing ceremony was also continued through the centuries. James II is believed to have been the last monarch to have performed it. The gifts were later replaced by the distribution of 'Maundy Money', in the form of silver coins specially minted for the purpose, which were given to a number of elderly and poor persons which tallied with the reigning monarch's age.

The distribution of Maundy Money continues to this day and is normally made at Westminster Abbey, although the ceremony has been conducted at Winchester Cathedral, and other locations. The coins are legal tender but the honour of receiving them from the king or queen is so great that it is rare for recipients to part with them, even though collectors are always willing to pay high prices.

Once in a blue moon is used to describe something which happens very rarely, such as the great volcanic eruption on the island of Krakatoa, between Sumatra and Java in Indonesia, in 1883. Rocks were hurled over 30 miles (48 km) high and the dust fell over 3,000 miles (4,800 km) away. It was said to be the greatest explosion since that of Santorini in the Aegean Sea, which occurred around 1470 BC, though the earlier one had been five times greater. During the Krakatoa eruption the volcanic dust in the atmosphere caused the moon to appear blue for some time.

The sulphur and dust particles from a forest fire, in 1950, which covered a large area along the Alaska Highway in northern Canada, also caused the moon to appear a bluish colour when it was observed from Great Britain.

Over the moon is to be delighted with something, or with the situation one finds oneself in. When people are extremely happy, or sportsmen achieve a victory, they frequently jump for joy, just as the cow did in the famous 18th-century nursery rhyme when it jumped over the moon. If a cow can do it, the implication is that humans can also. Such joy knows

[95]

no bounds and the moon, after all, is the earth's nearest neighbour in space, and is less than 250,000 miles (402,325 km) away, even when at its greatest distance from the earth.

His name is mud This saying originated when Abraham Lincoln, the sixteenth President of the USA, was assassinated in 1865. The man who shot Lincoln, John Wilkes Booth, broke a leg as he made his escape and was treated by a country doctor who knew nothing of what had happened. When Dr Samuel Mudd learnt of the assassination the following day, he immediately notified the authorities that the assassin and his patient must have been one and the same person. He was arrested, nevertheless, as a conspirator and sentenced to life imprisonment.

'His name is Mud' was thus coined (the second 'd' was dropped from the doctor's surname) by way of expressing contempt for him (and later referred to anyone whose actions or behaviour is bad).

Dr Mudd was later pardoned by Lincoln's successor (President Andrew Johnson) when he helped to stop an outbreak of yellow fever on the island where he was imprisoned.

During the 1970s, the descendants of Dr Mudd conducted a campaign with the White House to clear their ancestor's name. Although he had been officially pardoned, it was still implied that he had done something wrong. The doctor had taken the Hypocratic oath of service to humanity, like all members of his profession. He had tended a patient in need, and when he subsequently discovered that the man was a criminal he had informed the authorities. The original conviction had been unjust, the relatives reasoned, and should be declared null and void because the doctor had done nothing wrong.

To face the music is to stand up fearlessly in moments of difficulty and face the outcome. Professional speakers and actors often suffer from nerves when facing an audience, and big occasions frequently have bands in attendance. Actors and other performers making their entrance on stage not only have to face the audience, but also the music, i.e. the musicians in the orchestra positioned in front of the stage.

To nail one's colours to the mast is to make one's position and principles known and, then, stick to them by refusing to give way or climb down.

In the days of sail, if a crew was ready to surrender during a battle, the ship's flag (or colours) was hauled down. Many flags, however, were nailed to the mast by crews so that they could not be lowered, which meant that they had no intention of giving in and were ready to fight to the last, whatever the odds against them.

To pay on the nail is an expression still used to denote prompt payment, and arose from a practice in medieval markets, of great importance to the town and country folk for the buying and selling of their wares, produce and livestock. Quick justice was dealt out to those who broke agreements or cheated their customers. Eventually, it was decided that accounts must be settled at counters (short pillars and known as 'nails') in the open market, in the presence of witnesses.

Payments were placed on these pillars so that all and sundry could see that the money and change were correct, and that any bargains that had been made or offered were kept. Thus, the custom of 'paying on the nail' came into being.

For want of a nail Many a plan, or course of action, has been ruined 'for want of a nail'. The phrase served as a reminder that even the smallest detail, or the seemingly unimportant, must be thought of and checked, as it could prove vital to success. Just as a chain is only as strong as its weakest link, a kingdom can be lost for the want of a horseshoe nail, as Benjamin Franklin (1706–1790), the American statesman, scientist, inventor and writer, describes:

> For want of a nail the shoe was lost,
> For want of a shoe the horse was lost,
> For want of a horse the rider was lost,
> For want of a rider the battle was lost,
> For want of a battle the kingdom was lost;
> And all for the want of a horseshoe nail.

Nails, in a good state of preservation after thousands of years, have been found by archaeologists on a great many sites, in different parts of the world; this gives further proof that as long as we remember the 'nail', or smallest detail in a plan, it can be relied upon.

What's in a name? In early times people only had one name, and many of those names were taken from the Bible. Surnames, passed from father to son, did not come into widespread use until the 13th century. One name, or Christian name, was adequate until people came to live in communities in the towns and villages, then confusion arose when many people were found to have the same name. The problem was solved, to some extent, by adding a second name related to their various trades and occupations.

Many people were engaged in the metal trades, such as blacksmith, tinsmith and locksmith, and this is why such large numbers of people came to be called 'Smith'. Other popular trades included such names as Carpenter, Baker, Bell, Brewer, Butcher, Carter, Church, Cook, Miller, Shepherd, Turner, etc.

Surnames were also formed by using the names of the areas where people lived — York, Wells, Hall, Temple, Wood, Greenwood and Underwood, Brook, Burns, Cliff, Field, Ford, Hill, Moor, Stone, etc., as well as England, Scott, Welch, and Ireland. From colours there were names such as Black, Brown, Green, Gold, and White. Other names were formed from the seasons and points of the compass, such as Winter, Summer, North, South or Southey, East or Eastman, and West; and from animals, such as Martin, Nightingale, Peacock, Swan, Bull, Fox, Hart, Lyon (lion), and Lamb.

Sometimes the names came from personal characteristics — Little, Short, Long, Longman, Longfellow. Yet another choice was using 'the son of' from previous relatives' Christian names, e.g. Donaldson, Robinson, Wilson.

From the heyday of Medieval Chivalry we have Knight, and those who supported them: the Bowyer who made the bows; the Fletcher who made the arrows; Bannister who made cross-bows; and Boulter who made the bolts for them. At that time 'Esquire' was a legally recognized title of rank, immediately below that of knight; esquires served as the knight's shield-bearers. Esquire came to be used as a title in correspondence. It is still used today, though to a lesser extent, as 'Mr' is becoming more and more general.

Some surnames such as Prince, Lord and Bishop come from the 'nicknames' given to the people who played those roles in Medieval mystery plays performed in the towns and villages. Originally, 'nickname' was a word derived from 'eke name', which meant an additional name. Millers came to be known as 'Dusty' Miller; other connotations, such as 'Snowy' White, 'Dinger' Bell, 'Nobby' Clark, and 'Spud' Murphy continue to be used to this day.

Countries received nicknames too — 'John Bull' personifies the English nation, and 'Uncle Sam' (from the initials U.S.) represents the USA. Americans are also called 'Yankees', from 'Yengees', which was the nearest the Red Indians could get to pronouncing 'English'. Englishmen were called 'Limeys; this nickname originated in the old days of sail, when sea voyages took a long time and the food on board left a lot to be desired, and one of the perils that had to be faced was scurvy. This dreaded disease, caused by malnutrition and a lack of fresh fruit and vegetables containing vitamin C, is said to have caused the deaths of 10,000 sailors during Queen Elizabeth I's reign alone, and was still rife in many ships until just over a century ago. Scurvy caused blood spots to appear under a victim's skin, gums to bleed and teeth to fall out; sufferers rapidly became weak, and were totally exhausted by any sudden movement, and the slightest exertion frequently proved fatal.

The East India Company was granted a charter in 1600 by Elizabeth I and it pioneered the attack against scurvy by issuing lemon and lime juice to its seamen. Scurvy was reduced dramatically as their seamen, and later those of the shipping companies, and the Navy, continued to drink fruit juice as a precaution on their voyages around the world. British seamen came to be called 'lime-juicers' which, in time, became shortened to 'limey'.

Australians were nicknamed 'Aussie' or 'Digger', Irishmen 'Paddy', Welshmen 'Taffy', and the Scots were called 'Jock', 'Mac' or 'Sandy'.

Wars have produced their share of nicknames. To be sent back to 'Blighty' meant to return to England. Anyone who got a 'Blighty-one' had a wound severe enough to be sent back to England for treatment. 'Blighty' comes from the Hindi *bilayti*, meaning 'far away' and was first used by soldiers serving in India who were moved back home. British soldiers were nicknamed 'Tommy Atkins'. This name came from the account or record book shown to them to help fill in their details where the fictitious name of a Private Thomas Atkins, was used as a guide in the specimen entry. Sailors have long been known as 'Jack Tar', from the tar and tarpaulins used in ships during the days of sail.

A 'brass hat', which refers to an officer of high rank, dates from the First Boer War and is descriptive of the 'scrambled egg' or gold oak leaves on the peaks of their caps. World War II produced many nicknames, notably 'G.I.', for American private soldiers. As all their food and clothing was provided, the initials referred to 'Government Issue'. The all-purpose car used by the American officers and men, known as a 'Jeep' got its name from 'G.P.' – general purposes vehicle.

Amongst nicknames denoting affection, we have 'Darby and Joan' used to describe old married couples. Its origin is from an 18th-century ballad written about John Darby and his wife Joan, who lived to a ripe old age in Yorkshire and remained devoted to each other throughout their long married life. Still on affection, but of a different variety, we have 'a Casanova', which applies to an unfaithful lover who has relationships with many women. The name is from Giovanni Casanova, the 18th-century Venetian adventurer, who wrote the memoirs of his eventful life and many love affairs. Similarly, a 'Don Juan' is based on the 17th-century Spanish literary character, who was also famous for his many love affairs.

Other derogatory nicknames include 'gaffer', used as a term of contempt for an old labourer, but formerly to denote respect, being a corruption of 'grandfather'. Nowadays it is sometimes used to describe the boss of a business. Alternatively, he might be called 'Mr Big' — the man in control but who remains unknown. 'A Scrooge' isn't much use to himself or anyone else, being a miser who hoards and counts his money over and over again, spending little and who refrains from taking part in the things other people enjoy. This unpleasant character appears in *A Christmas Carol* by Charles Dickens.

'Box and Cox' is descriptive of an ingenious arrangement which manages to obtain the maximum advantages from the least possible resources. This phrase originated from a farce of that name, written in the 19th century, in which a lodging-house landlady let the same room to two men, Box and Cox, one of whom was out at work all day, and the other at night and, thus, never met.

Many people think that 'Superman' is a modern nickname for a person of super-human qualities of intellect and physique, but the term was invented by Nietzsche, the German 19th-century philosopher and essayist.

A number of things in everyday use have obtained their names from the surnames of people who made them famous. John Montagu, the 4th Earl of Sandwich (1718–1792), was said to be so addicted to gambling that he had no time to stop for regular meals. Instead, he got his servant to place meat between slices of bread so that he could eat at the gaming table during sessions which sometimes lasted for twenty-four hours, thus giving his name to the 'sandwich' which has since become so popular for snacks and quick meals. An alternative account states that John Montagu was not obsessed with cards and gaming, but a hard-working politician, and First Lord of the Admiralty between 1771–1782, who took his duties so seriously that he ate 'sandwiches' to enable him to continue his work on State affairs without leaving his desk.

The short over-jacket known as a 'spencer' worn by men, as well as women, which is back in fashion now, came into being when the 2nd Earl of Spencer (1758–1834) first wore one. Another Peer, the 7th Earl of Cardigan, made the knitted woollen over-waistcoat popular and gave his name to the 'cardigan' around the middle of the 19th century.

Writers often make use of a pseudonym, or pen name to conceal their identity. William Makepeace Thackeray (1811–1863), one of the most brilliant of English novelists and author of five major novels, including *Vanity Fair* and *The Virginians*, also wrote poems, and some of his earlier works were written not under one pen name, but many: 'Michael Angelo Titmarsh', 'Charles James Yellowplush', 'George Savage Fitzboodle', 'Arthur Pendennis', 'Theophilus Wagstaff', and others, including 'Dorothea Julia Ramsbottom'.

Caught napping is to be found asleep, and taken unawares. 'Nap' comes from the Saxon *knappian* meaning to doze, or sleep lightly or briefly, especially by day. Such short naps are also known as 'cat naps' as cats frequently indulge in them, but several other animals have this habit, and can be said to have been 'caught napping' while doing so.

Many birds have been observed flying far out at sea at night; when these birds have to fly over vast areas of sea, where they cannot land, they stay on the wing all night. Some birds have been observed to fly without landing for between 60 and 90 hours, and they even 'cat nap' during flight.

To work like a navvy implies that one has worked hard on a job and put everything one has got into it in terms of a great deal of effort and sweat.

The word 'navvy' used to refer to labourers employed in excavating canals. The canals were known as navigations, and the men who dug them were called navigators — 'navvy' being a contraction.

Between the mid-18th and mid-19th centuries no fewer than 4,700 miles of canals were cut in England. The term navvy later came to be used for any labourer excavating railways and, subsequently, roads.

Many countries have canals which are used for irrigation as well as transportation. Some of them are many hundreds of miles long.

To grasp the nettle is to attack a difficult situation, or problem, boldly — it is a saying which has been used for centuries.

The nettle has for long had a bad reputation and been cursed by gardeners and country people for its hairs which, when touched or brushed against, secrete an acrid liquid that stings the skin. However, its reputation is undeserved for it has rendered valuable service to mankind through the ages — as food, in medicinal cures for many ailments, and as a fabric for sheets and tablecloths. Nettles cause no pain or difficulties when handled firmly, as suggested by the poem of Aaron Hill (1685–1750):

> Tender-handed stroke a nettle,
> And it strings you for your pains;
> Grasp it like a man of mettle,
> And it soft as silk remains.

In the nick of time means only just in time, at the eleventh hour, as it were. 'Nick' is a modified form of 'nock' or 'notch'. The phrase arose from the old practice of marking time and transactions by scoring notches on a stick, known as a tally. (*See* 'To keep a TALLY'). Today, the expression is often used to indicate anyone who is saved from some predicament at the critical moment, or who settles an account, or pays a bill, in time but at the very last moment.

Up to the nines To be dressed in this way means to be dressed elaborately. In its other sense, it can refer to having a great deal of work on hand while reaching out as nearly as possible to perfection. In former times the 'nines' alluded to classical scholars seeking this perfection through learning — represented by the Nine Muses of Greek and Roman mythology. Three of the Muses were supposed to inspire the various passions of poetry, while the remaining six presided over history, comedy, tragedy, music, dancing, and astronomy.

No names, no pack drill Of 20th-century origin, this phrase is derived from a form of punishment in the British Army in which an offender against military discipline was made to march up and down smartly with a heavy pack on his back.

The phrase warns against mentioning names when some serious mistake has been made, or when a confidential issue is under discussion, and the speaker wishes to withold the name of the people involved who might suffer if it became publicly known.

To pour oil on troubled waters is to calm down a difficult situation by soothing words or actions. It is a well-known fact that an area of rough sea can be made calmer by pouring oil on the surface. The Venerable Bede mentions this in his *Ecclesiastical History*, of 731 AD, when he wrote that St Aidan gave a young priest a cruse of oil to pour on the sea in case a storm blew up while he was escorting a maiden who was destined to become the bride of King Oswin. When a storm did arise, the priest poured the oil on the rough sea and it became calm.

Although modern seamen still, on occasions, discharge oil on to troubled water, the phrase did not come into everyday use until the 19th century — notably through the writings of Charles Kingsley in *Westward Ho!*

One to show, one to blow was used until comparatively recent times to imply that all was not what it seemed, and that one had something out of sight in reserve. Its origin is from the practice of well-dressed men to wear a handkerchief (white or coloured) in the breast-pocket of their jacket for show, and had a second one in another pocket of their clothing, which was the one they actually used.

At one time, handkerchiefs were available in many different sizes. For the last 200 years, however, they have come in only one shape — square. This came about through the royal decree of Marie Antoinette which declared that, for practical purposes, the length and breadth of handkerchiefs should be equal.

Know one's onions *see* To KNOW the ropes

Paddle *see* To paddle your own CANOE

A parting shot, or Parthian shot is a final cutting remark, or severe glance of disapproval, given by one person to another as they part after an argument or meeting. The timing is such that it leaves one's opponent or rival no time in which to reply or react.

The phrase is derived from Western Asia; the favourite tactics of the ancient Parthians were to discharge missiles and arrows backwards whenever their horsemen and soldiers were retreating from the enemy, hence, 'Parthian shot', or shaft.

You pays your money and you takes your choice This line appeared in *Punch* in 1846. It suggests that when faced with a choice between two similar possibilities, or alternatives, one might just as well rely on luck. It is still used by traders with market stalls, and the rhyme in full is:

> What ever you please my little dears:
> You pays your money and you takes your choice.
> You pays your money and what you sees is
> A cow or a donkey just as you pleases.

(*See* 'Hobson's choice'.)

He who pays the piper calls the tune In medieval times, when strolling musicians toured the country, pipers expected to be paid by the members of the audience for the entertainment they gave in inns and at village gatherings. Whoever gave them money had the right to choose which tune they should play. When the phrase is used today it serves as a reminder that whoever puts up the money or pays for something has control over the way in which the money is used.

Pecking order Birds, like human beings, live in a competitive society. There is usually one bird which dominates all the rest through superior aggressiveness, while other birds are only able to dominate birds immediately below them in the hierarchy. Each bird knows which birds it can expect to be pecked by, and which it can peck.

To understand the 'pecking order' in human society is to know one's place, and that of other people.

A peeping Tom is a person who obtains pleasure from peeping out of lewd curiosity, at things which he shouldn't, in particular at women undressing.

The expression goes back to the middle of the 11th century when Leofric, Earl of Mercia, established a Benedictine monastery, around which the town (and later the city) of Coventry developed. Within a short time, the Earl had levied such a high tax that the people would have starved if they had paid it. After a continuous barrage of protests from the public, Leofric said he would only lift the tax if his wife, Lady Godiva, rode naked through the streets.

Sympathetic to their cause, Lady Godiva agreed. She made the condition imposed by her husband known so that the townsfolk should keep within their homes behind drawn or shuttered blinds. Only one man 'Peeping Tom', a tailor, ventured to look out as she rode by, and he was struck blind.

The pen is mightier than the sword implies that the written word can be more powerful, and more to be feared, than physical force. During the time of Elizabeth I's reign, the only way that news and opinions could be circulated was through pamphlets passed from hand to hand, but when these were banned, and all printing presses outside London, Oxford and Cambridge, had to be registered, unauthorized presses still continued to operate and get round the official censorship, despite the penalties.

The official view, through many successive reigns, was that the public should only be allowed to read what the government of the day wanted them to read. The only official publication offered was *The London Gazette* (originally *The Oxford Gazette*) which did just that, and was first published in 1665. The first newspaper which could freely express any opinion first appeared in 1702, at the beginning of Queen Anne's reign.

William Caxton set up the first press in England over two and a quarter centuries previously, after learning the art of printing in Germany. He printed nearly eighty books before he died in 1491. Caxton was also an author who wrote a book on Chess, another on the story of Troy, as well as twenty-one translations of other works.

The first book ever produced by mechanical means in North America was the *Bay Psalm Book*, printed in 1640. Only about two copies exist in reasonable condition. The oldest mechanically printed book in the world is believed to be what is known as the *Gutenberg Bible*, printed in Mainz, Germany, *c.*1454–1455. When three of the few copies which still exist were put up for sale in 1978 the University of Texas bought one for $2,400,000 (£1,265,000) which, at that time, was the highest price ever known to have been paid for a book.

Lead in your pencil is an expression used when a drink or other stimulant is offered to enable one to carry out some strenuous activity.

Pencils, in fact, do not contain lead but a compound mineral substance called *plumbago*, found in masses or lumps between layers of slate, which came into use for this purpose in England during the last half of the 16th century. The high quality of English drawing-pencils means they are sought after everywhere and the mine for this material, at Borrowdale, in Cumberland, is considered the finest in the world. Its produce was so valuable, in fact, that it was only opened once in every four to seven years, and in one hour a single workman could obtain £2,000 worth. After a sufficient quantity had been obtained, the mine was carefully secured again.

Later, the mine was opened every year to keep pace with demand. Then, just as it was feared that the supply would soon run out, large deposits of plumbago of a pure quality were found in Siberia, and subsequently in other parts of the world.

Originally, lead was used for marking and drawing since the days of the Romans, before plumbago or graphite was used in pencils, and the name still sticks.

In for a penny, in for a pound *see* May as well be HANGED for a sheep as a lamb

Hoist with his own petard The petard was an ancient engine of war, fired with gunpowder, which was used to demolish obstacles and blow in such things as strongly constructed doors. It was frequently hoisted up to destroy obstacles at a high level; but it was such an infernal machine that anyone who had the unfortunate task of firing it stood in great danger of losing their own life.

The phrase, thus, came to be used to describe anyone who is caught in their own trap, or who is ruined by their own devices against others.

To peter out When something peters out it has stopped, or come to an end. The phrase arose in the American goldfields during the first half of the 19th century, when the two principal methods of mining gold were used. 'Placer' mining, which had been known since ancient times, was the easiest because nature had already done most of the work, eroding and leaching gold-bearing rocks into a fine powder, or into nuggets which could be separated from the alluvial deposits in prospectors' pans. The Great Californian Gold Rush started with the discovery of placer gold. The other method was known as 'lode' mining, in which the gold had to be extracted from solid rock.

Peter is Greek for rock, and can also refer to a vein of ore. When a seam had been worked to exhaustion and revealed no more gold, it was said to have 'petered out'. Peter also obtains its name from the saltpetre of the explosive in the gunpowder used to extract and break up the gold-bearing rocks into a workable size.

Many prospectors often mistook the brassy yellow colour they discovered in veins and seams for the real thing, and fell victim to what came to be known as 'fool's gold', which subsequently gave rise to the warning that 'all that glitters is not gold', meaning that one should not judge anything by its attractive appearance alone as it might not turn out to be what it seems.

A **stormy petrel** describes someone whose approach portends trouble. Petrels are small sea birds, with black and white plumage and long wings, associated by sailors with bringing rough weather. Their Italian name *Petrello* (little Peter) is related to their curious method of flight in which they skim over the waves, patting the surface of the water with each foot alternately as they go, giving the impression that they are walking on it, just as St Peter did on the Sea of Galilee. Sailors know them as Mother Carey's chickens and, despite this domesticated image, these little birds spend most of their life over the open seas and can ride out Atlantic winter hurricanes. They return to land only to breed.

To rise from the ashes like a phoenix is often used to describe a favourable development from what appeared to be an impossible or ruinous situation.

According to Greek mythology, the phoenix was a fabulous sacred bird, supposed to live for 500 or 600 years in the deserts of Arabia. As death approached, she built herself a nest of spices on an altar, sang a melodious dirge, and then set light to the pyre by fanning it with her wings. The flames reduced her to ashes, from which she arose, full of youth and vigour, to a new life.

The phoenix, a symbol of immortality, was unique, and another phrase 'as rare as the phoenix' was used frequently by writers during the

16th century. Shakespeare mentions the phoenix many times in his plays, and in *Henry VIII* (5. 5):

> Nor shall this peace sleep with her; but as when
> The bird of wonder dies, the maiden phoenix,
> Her ashes new-create another heir
> As great in admiration as herself.

Pig in the middle Anyone in this situation is unlikely to be envied for he will be in a position between two people, or groups of people, opposed to each other, whom no one takes any notice of and who is powerless to influence things one way or the other. The phrase comes from the once-popular childrens' game in which the child standing between the opposing players was called 'pig in the middle', and everyone tried to prevent them from getting hold of the ball, catching the players, or having any influence on the outcome of the game.

A pig in a poke If something is said to be 'a pig in a poke' this is a warning to have a close look at what you are buying before you part with your money. Frauds were frequently carried out in the old-time markets when a young pig was put on display, and the seller was supposed to be offering others tied in sacks (pokes) ready for carrying away. When those who bought them got home, instead of a sucking-pig they found a cat.

Anyone not a simpleton would insist on opening the bag in the market before buying. If the trader was dishonest the buyer would '*let the cat out of the bag*'. This became an expression which was in itself a revelation of a secret or trick, either deliberately or accidentally, and usually at the worst possible moment.

A pigeon pair Pigeons, which were probably the first birds to be domesticated by man, only lay two eggs which, it is said, hatch into one male and one female — hence the expression 'a pigeon pair'. This is sometimes used to describe boy and girl twins, or a family consisting of one boy and one girl as sole children.

As plain as a pikestaff Two origins are suggested for this phrase, which denotes anything obvious and easy to understand. One of them draws attention to the fact that the pikestaffs used in weaponry had extremely long shafts and would therefore be easy to see. The alternative suggestion reminds us that the pikestaff was originally the 'packstaff' used by pedlars on which they carried their pack, and which was worn 'plain' (or smooth) from continual use.

Pin *see* Pin MONEY

It's in the pipeline *see* Don't CALL us, we'll call you

Plumbing the depths *see* Swinging the LEAD

Pocket *see* LINING the pocket

To mind your Ps and Qs is a warning to be polite, and careful of one's actions and behaviour. It is usually said to the young but, originally, was probably directed at printers to remind them to be careful of these two letters of the alphabet in case they were mixed or placed upside-down when setting up type.

Alternatively, it could have been a warning to customers in public houses to mind their Ps (pints) and Qs (quarts) when these were 'chalked up' and would eventually have to be paid for.

Yet another explanation for the phrase is said to come from French court etiquette, in the days when large wigs were fashionable. The 'P' was the French *pied* or foot, and the 'Q' — *le queue* — the hanging plaited tail of a wig. In this case the admonition was to remind young and old alike to be careful where they put their feet, to keep them together and to bow slowly and gracefully so that their wigs would not get entangled with others, or fall off.

To tell someone point blank is to do so directly by going straight to the point and speaking explicitly. The phrase originates from the French *point blanc* which refers to the white spot in the centre of a target. If an arrow, or other missile, is to achieve the maximum effect it must not deviate, but go straight to the bull's-eye.

Port *see* Any port in a STORM

Posh A jet flight to India or the Far East today takes a matter of hours. By contrast, the same journey on an ocean liner in the past could take as many weeks. The privileged, of course, always chose to travel as comfortably as possible on the longer sea voyages; the cabins most in demand were the coolest ones on the Far East run — those facing north. So, the best and most expensive cabins to book were those on the port side outward, and on the starboard side home. The shipping lines abbreviated this booking procedure of the wealthy to POSH, and the expression has long been used to describe smart, tiptop people.

To play possum is to pretend to be ill, asleep, or oblivious of what is going on around one. The phrase comes from the ability of one of the marsupials, the Virginia Opossum of North America, to avoid capture by feigning death when threatened or being attacked.

Marsupials obtain their name from the Latin word for pouch, in which the females carry their young. Kangaroos are members of the marsupial family but the opossum is much smaller — about the size of a cat. The female often bear as many as twenty young each year which are so tiny at birth that it is said that they could all fit into a tablespoon. Not all survive but those that do manage to crawl, even though blind, into their mother's pouch where they suckle for sixty days or so. When they are sufficiently developed to leave the pouch they are still reliant on their mother, climbing on her back to be carried around for several weeks. Sometimes the mother holds her tail over her back so that each of the young can wrap their own tail around it for greater security as she moves around.

When the mother considers the young are sufficiently grown to look after themselves she shakes them loose. Her long rat-like tail has many uses, and also serves as a fifth hand to grasp objects, such as the branches of trees, enabling her to climb with great agility. The opossum also has thumbed hind-feet which enable it to grasp objects much in the same way as we use our hands.

Despite these advantages, as well as sharp teeth and claws, the opossum is not very well equipped for defence against enemies, except for one thing . . . its ability to 'play possum'. When threatened it immediately goes into a coma. Its eyes close and its body goes limp. It does this so effectively that many of its predators turn away believing it to be dead. Even if it is picked up by its tail and prodded, it remains motionless. The moment the danger is past, however, the 'dead' opossum revives instantly and runs away as fast as it can go.

To go post-haste is to go (or do anything) as quickly as possible. The phrase was used in England during the early 16th century. The reference is to the post-horse system in which a series of men were stationed at intervals along the roads to carry the letters in relays from one point to the next. There were fresh horses at each change-over and, thus, the post went with the maximum haste.

A subsequent development of this system in America led to the formation of the famous 'Pony Express' which came into being in 1860 to carry first-class mail from St Joseph, Missouri, to Sacramento, California, close to the Pacific coast — a distance of almost 2,000 miles (3,218 km). The scheduled time for the whole journey was ten days, which meant that 200 miles (322 km) had to be covered every twenty-four hours. Relay stations were set up every 10 to 15 miles (16 to 24 km) where a blacksmith and two men were stationed to look after the horses in readiness.

Each rider originally rode four stages, but this was later increased to eight. The change-over from one horse to another, and transfer of the mail pouch to the next saddle, had to be completed within two-and-a-half minutes, though some managed it in less than half this time. The road conditions were rough and each horse was ridden at full gallop from one stage to the next. The riders were armed but were under orders only to fight when absolutely necessary, relying on speed to elude any possible attackers. During the eighteen months in which the Pony Express operated, when it was replaced by the railroad, only one mail pouch was lost in an ambush.

Among the riders was a young teenager named Cody, who subsequently became a scout for the US Army and fought in the Civil War. Cody was later famous the world over as 'Buffalo Bill', and founder of the celebrated 'Wild West' show with which he toured America and Europe. Bill Cody died in 1917. His grave, in a vault on the top of the rocky Lookout Mountain, Colorado, is still a famous tourist attraction.

The pot calling the kettle black is used to describe anyone who blames another for faults which they also have. The 17th-century phrase is based on the fact that pots and kettles would both be blackened, like any other cooking utensils, after long use over an open fire; neither, therefore, had the right to criticize the other.

Gone to pot refers to anything which has gone to ruin, or which is beyond repair. The phrase comes from the melting-pots into which broken items of metal, gold and silver, were thrown when they could no longer be used in their original form as they were either damaged, or stolen.

To take pot luck When anyone is invited to take pot luck it means that they cannot expect a special meal to be prepared to celebrate their arrival, and that they will be welcome to share whatever food is available, or in the pot that day. The expression stems from the days of open fireplaces when a pot was always kept boiling on the fire. It was usually hung above the fire on the long arm of an iron bracket fixed to a side wall of the chimney. When wood for burning became short during the 17th century, coal was substituted and soon became more popular as it supplied a more even and controllable heat source.

If one was invited to 'take a dry stew', on the other hand, that meant something entirely different. For although water was plentiful, its use was restricted by its inaccessibility and lack of purity. The rich cleansed it by boiling before drinking it, and they were also able to indulge in the luxury of taking baths in wooden vats. Those who were poorer, and less fortunate in not having a convenient water source nearby, had to go to special 'houses', set up by the authorities, where they could take what was known as a 'dry stew', in which they sat on a stool, in a vat beside hot stones, over which cold water was poured every now and again.

Press ganged into it To 'press gang' anyone, or an organization, today is to bring extreme pressure to bear in forcing one's way, or idea, on them and compelling them to accept it and, therefore, into doing something against their will. Originally, it referred to the compulsory enlistment of men into the Navy.

In former times men living near the English coasts went in fear of the dreaded press gangs, led by former naval officers, armed with clubs and a warrant which entitled them to seize men and force them to serve in the Navy, where the conditions, pay and food were appalling, and shore-leave almost non-existent.

Victims were faced with enemies all round — from the press gangs who were paid to do the job by way of a commission payment, to the land folk who were either women or men too old to be subject to 'impress', who were bribed with handsome rewards for reporting any deserting seaman to the authorities.

The few victims who did manage to escape from their ships faced the severest of penalties when recaptured and, at the beginning of the 19th century, four men who were caught were sentenced to be 'flogged through the fleet', which involved receiving twenty-five lashes from a 'cat o' nine tails' at each ship. (*See* 'not enough room to swing a CAT'.)

None but the strongest or the brave could imagine being able to withstand such punishment, let alone witness it, and many a sailor would have preferred to have been sentenced to death.

Most captains preferred volunteers for their ships, but during the Dutch Wars of the 17th century the Navy's strength had to be increased by 27,000 men, most of whom were press ganged into service. The press gangs were finally phased out two hundred years later after the Napoleonic Wars of 1796–1815.

To maintain a low profile Originally a profile was an outline drawing, or silhouette of the human face, usually when seen in side view. The word comes from the Italian *profilo*, and Latin *filum*, meaning a thread. In more recent years the profile was extended to cover a written, or filmed, portrayal of a person which appeared in the press, or on television. When anyone, particularly if they are in the public eye, wants to avoid publicity or escape being questioned, they 'maintain a low profile' in order to avoid being seen, or attracting attention. Companies engaged on the development of new products, or processes, also maintain a low profile in order to avoid any leakage of their secrets to competitors.

Promise *see* A LICK and a promise

Pull *see* To pull out all the STOPS

To be in quad (quod) — QED and QEF To be in 'quad' is a contraction of quadrangle, a four-sided court, partly enclosed or fully surrounded by buildings. When boys at public schools, or undergraduates at university were confined to it they were referred to as being 'in quad'.

When spelt as 'quod' it refers to the exercise yard of prisons, surrounded by buildings and walls, in which debtors were allowed to receive visitors. The alternative phrase 'to be in' or 'out of quod' was not only confined to prisons, but gave rise to a phrase often used (though seldom currently) by schoolboys whose financial position (pocket money) was either nil, or inadequate.

The Latin phrase *quod erat demonstrandum* meaning 'which was to be

[113]

shown', was first used in its abbreviated form 'QED' at the end of theorems in geometry, and meant that they had been proved.

'QEF' — *quod erat faciendum* — on the other hand, was used when the calculations or points had yet to be made or shown. Both abbreviated forms are still in general use today.

To be in queer street is to be in debt, or financial difficulties, and is supposed to have arisen from the practice of tradesmen who put a 'query', or question mark beside the name of a customer whose credit-worthiness they doubted.

Until just over 200 years ago debtors were still being treated more severely than thieves and hardened criminals. Once imprisoned they could stay locked up for the rest of their lives amidst the most appalling conditions of filth, vice, and brutality from their jailers. The only way out was by paying their debts, which was virtually impossible because anyone in a position to do this would have been able to avoid being imprisoned in the first place. Once inside, they had no way of earning any money and they often faced life imprisonment for debts of a little over £1. This state of affairs persisted until 1776, when an Act of Parliament was introduced to free all debtors who had been imprisoned before that date.

In more recent times, anyone who was insolvent was liable to find themselves not only in 'Queer Street', but in 'Carey Street', the street in London which used to house the bankruptcy court.

Question *see* The name of the GAME

To be on the qui vive means to be on the alert, attentive and watchful. It comes from the French phrase meaning 'Who goes there?' which is the sentry's challenge to anyone approaching while on guard.

Quiz *see* the name of the GAME

Rack and ruin The rack in this phrase has nothing to do with the ancient instrument of torture, but with driving clouds and winds and a consequent shipwreck. The meaning becomes more obvious if one knows that 'rack' is a variant of 'wreck', (formerly spelt 'wrack'). It is used to describe loss of fortune.

What a way to run a railway This phrase has been used since the turn of the century but became widely popular as the result of a cartoon which appeared in the American magazine *Ballyhoo* in 1932, portraying a signalman looking out of his signal-box at two trains careering along the same line towards each other. As he watches them about to collide head on he says, 'Tch-Tch — what a way to run a railway!'

The phrase gained even wider popularity after the screening of the comedy film *Man in the Moon*, in which the British actor Kenneth More was engaged by a professor working on a project to rocket a team of 'supermen' to the moon. Kenneth More played the part of a man who never worries and who appears to be completely immune from anger, hate, greed, and fear. (The actual landing on the moon by the American astronaut Neil Armstrong, did not take place until some years later, in 1969.) Kenneth More imagined his role only required him to match his reactions to those of the astronauts, in the film, whom he thinks are test pilots.

After the most gruelling and rigorous tests, which he comes through with flying colours, we see him in yet another test strapped into a seat mounted on wheels and catapulted along a railway track until it is stopped abruptly by buffers at the end of the track. The 'G' (gravity) force is so great that his body bursts through the safety harness, hurling him high in the air to land in a reservoir. As he struggles back and lifts his head and shoulders above the parapet his immortal words 'What a way to run a railway!' became one of the greatest understatements of all time.

Today we still use the phrase to describe chaotic conditions, or a thoroughly disorganized way of doing things.

As right as rain means that someone, or something, is all right or in an excellent state. It can apply to a person's health, position, or circumstances, to an opinion which is considered to be quite sound, or to the state of some object. The original phrase was 'as right as a trivet', which was in use during the early 19th century, and 'as right as rain' superceded it towards the close of the century. The connection between the two does not become clear until the original meanings of the words 'right' and 'trivet' are understood. 'Right' meant 'steady'. (Without having a great deal of weather knowledge in those days, they must have assumed that when it rained it did so steadily.) A 'trivet' was a tripod-like stand which remained steady on its three legs, as it supported cooking vessels by the fire in the correct upright position.

It never rains but it pours — The pot of gold at the end of the rainbow 'When two Englishmen meet, their first talk is of the weather' wrote Dr Samuel Johnson, the most celebrated English literary figure of the 18th century. When 2 inches (51 mm) of rain fell in 12 minutes at Wisbech, in Cambridgeshire on 28 June 1970, the residents talked of nothing else for it was the most intense rainfall ever recorded in Britain by scientific methods.

For over a thousand years, the English have watched eagerly to see if it rains on the 15 July, St Swithin's Day. Although St Swithin was a builder of churches and of public works, and the bishop of Winchester, he disliked pomp and was a man of unusual piety and humility. When he was dying in 862 AD he asked to be buried in the common graveyard at Winchester where pedestrians might pass over his head, and where the rain could fall on him. His wish was carried out, but when the monks decided a few years later that the great saint deserved a better tomb and attempted to remove his remains to within the church on 15 July, violent rains made it impossible and continued to pour from the sky for the next forty days.

The task of removal was not attempted again for a century, until 963 AD, when it was successful, but by then St Swithin's Day had become established as an omen of bad weather with the belief, still currently held, that if it rains on 15 July it will continue to do so for forty days.

The phrase IT NEVER RAINS BUT IT POURS is of much later origin in the 18th century, but it makes use of the St Swithin's Day analogy by implying that when things go wrong, they have a habit of continuing to do so for some time, and one event, or misfortune, is followed closely by another.

This is enough to send victims in search of the legendary POT OF GOLD

AT THE END OF THE RAINBOW. Despite ancient belief that if one digs into the ground where a rainbow touches the earth, one will be sure to find a crock, or pot, of gold, the phrase is still used of 'rainbow-chasers' — people who search for imaginary wealth.

Raining cats and dogs

> I like the weather, when it is not rainy,
> That is, I like two months of every year.

So wrote Lord George Gordon Byron (1788–1824) the famous English poet. Although rain is essential, most of us complain about it, and when it 'rains cats and dogs' we have every reason to do so. The phrase dates from at least the mid-17th century and implies that in the severest of rainfalls one can expect every possible thing to fall out of the sky.

In old Norse weather lore, the cat is associated with storms, and the dog with the wind and, although one of these weather elements is usually accompanied by the other, cats and dogs certainly do not fall out of the sky, though fish and frogs have done so on many occasions in different countries.

Dismissing the many tales in folklore about such happenings, more scientific explanations suggest that fish and frogs can be lifted by waterspouts which then deposit them some distance away. There are many authentic accounts, substantiated by experts, in which fish and frogs have fallen in heavy rainstorms into gardens, and on to a Hampshire golf course, in England, witnessed by several members, who were not observing the phenomenon from the 19th hole.

Not worth a rap is anything that is worthless. When small coins became scarce in Ireland, in the 1720s, a base halfpenny, known as a 'rap', was put in circulation. They were only worth about half a farthing and were virtually without value.

Ready when you are This phrase originated during the heyday of Hollywood spectaculars, when some scenes could only be filmed once, due to the danger or the mammoth cast involved. To make sure that the events were captured on film, several camera crews were used to film the scene from different positions — the film directors took the view that a result was certain because there was 'safety in numbers'.

The method is still used, particularly where films have to be made on low budgets. A documentary film was made of an RAF V-bomber landing, with the undercarriage up, on a carpet of foam sprayed on the runway. The aircraft was an old one and there was no further use for it, but there was no likelihood of another aircraft being available for some years. The object of the exercise was to show that aircraft could be landed on a carpet of foam, when their undercarriages were jammed in the retracted position, without injury to the crew and occupants, if done correctly. However, the filming obviously couldn't be repeated and had to be right first time.

The film director had taken the precaution of using three different cameramen, positioned behind protective sandbags at strategic points close to and alongside the foamed runway. As the aircraft approached, it was throttled back and set in a shallow glide; the fuselage made contact with the runway precisely opposite camera one, cushioned along the foam past camera two, and came to a halt right in front of camera three.

When the film director called up camera one, over the radio-link, to find out how things had gone, the cameraman said his film had jammed. The director called camera two, to be told that the focus-pull had stuck. The director turned his binoculars towards his final hope. The operator was crouched out of sight with the lens trained exactly in the right direction through a slit in the sandbags.

'Camera Three — how about you?'

'Ready when you are!'

This enthusiastic but useless reply has caught on outside the film industry, and when it is used in general conversation it means the exact opposite to what it says. In other words 'You go ahead — don't count on me'.

Reason *see* Ours not to reason WHY

Red letter day is a day on which something good or notable happens, or which is remembered as the date of some joyful occurrence. The expression arises from the saint's days and festivals which are often marked in red letters on calendars, instead of black.

Like a red rag to a bull means to provoke, anger, or annoy. The phrase is based on the widely-held belief that the red cloth waved by bullfighters in Spain enraged the bulls so much that it made them attack. This is totally without foundation, however, as modern scientific research has shown that bulls are colour-blind. Tests have also demonstrated that when other coloured cloths are used the bulls are equally enraged, for it is the movement, and not the colour, which makes them angry and prompts them to attack.

[118]

Red tape This phrase is said to have been invented by Charles Dickens; it is still used to describe the excessive and rigid adherence to regulations and time-wasting formalities in public business. The phrase refers to the colour of the tape used to secure bundles of official and legal documents, though pink, rather than red, would have been a more accurate description.

Ride roughshod over To do this to someone, or a group of people or an organization, is to take the reins in one's own hands and go ahead with a course of action, without any consideration for the feelings or interests of others. The phrase comes from the days when it was common practice to ride rough-shod horses in which the nail-heads of the horseshoes were left projecting so that they could be ridden anywhere without slipping, particularly in icy conditions.

The rift within the lute refers to a small integral flaw in something, or some organization, which prevents it from being perfect or able to achieve its objective, and usually implies stupidity or dissension from within.

The lute, which was an ancient, pear-shaped, stringed instrument of Arabian origin, required the greatest craftsmanship in its making from carefully selected wood. The slightest flaw could develop into a crack with the inevitable result, as described by Tennyson:

> It is the little rift within the lute
> That by and by will make the music mute,
> And, ever widening, slowly silence all.

Although it was the most difficult of stringed instruments to play, it was very popular from the 14th to 17th centuries, particularly during Elizabethan times. A considerable amount of music was composed specially for the lute, either to accompany songs or to play solos.

Fra Angelico's famous painting *Coronation of the Virgin* shows Angels using both methods of playing the lute, with one figure using fingers to pluck the strings, and another using a bow.

What a rigmarole A 'rigmarole' is a corruption of 'Ragman Roll', which was a long document presented to Edward I (1272–1307) by loyal Scottish noblemen when he visited them. The noblemen paid homage to him by signing individual deeds. These were incorporated, with many pendant seals, into the single document, which measured 40 ft (12 m) long.

[119]

The expression 'what a rigmarole' has been used since the early eighteenth century to describe a long, rambling and confused talk, or tale, or repetitive documents containing a dull catalogue of words and events.

The Ragman Role is housed in the Public Records Office with the nation's State papers, records and documents, which date from the time of the Norman Conquest. They include the Doomsday Book of 1086.

Ring see To ring the CHANGES

To read the riot act — To frog march The Riot Act refers to an English law, over 250 years old, which made it unlawful for a dozen or more persons to gather for riotous, or other illegal purposes. Anyone remaining after the relevant part of the Act had been read officially was guilty of felony. Once such an unruly person was arrested he was usually 'frog-marched' off to custody, carried face downwards by four men, each holding an arm or leg, with his body horizontal to the ground, in a manner in which he could offer the least resistance.

When people today receive a severe reprimand from their boss, or superior, they might return to their colleagues and say that they had just had the riot act read to them. Parents, too, often threaten children causing a commotion that if they don't behave themselves, they will have the riot act read to them, implying that after this they will have to face the full consequences of their misbehaviour.

Rise from the ashes see to rise from the ashes like a PHOENIX

To be sold down the river is an expression still used frequently today, particularly by groups of workers who feel that they have been betrayed or let down by the officials whom they elected to represent their interests. The river originally referred to was the Mississippi at the time when American owners sold domestic slaves to plantation owners down the river where the living and working conditions were usually extremely harsh.

Robbing Peter to pay Paul is to borrow money from one source, or person, in order to give it to another to repay a debt. All one has done is to incur another debt without improving one's financial position.

The phrase is commonly associated with the abbey church of St Peter, Westminster, which was created a cathedral in 1550 but lost this status ten years later and was rejoined to the diocese of London. Many of its estates were appropriated to the repairs of St Paul's cathedral, and the abbey lost what St Paul's had gained.

When St Paul's was destroyed in the Great Fire of London just over 100 years later, in 1666, and redesigned by Sir Christopher Wren, the one thing lacking was money. A tax on all coal coming into London enabled work to begin in 1675, but when this money ran out Wren managed to persuade the Government to treble the coal tax.

While the cathedral was being built, Wren made frequent trips in a wicker-basket, hauled up the scaffolding on a rope, to see how the work was progressing. By the time it was completed in 1710, five-sixths of all the money needed to build it had been raised from the tax on coal.

Ropes *see* to KNOW the ropes

A round robin is a written petition, or protest, which is drawn up and circulated for signature by a group with a common cause. Nowadays the signatures are usually written one beneath the other, but in former times they were arranged in a circle so that no name headed the list, and no one appeared as the ringleader or originator of the protest. The robin does not refer to the bird but *rond*, the French for round, and *ruban*, the French for ribbon.

Before one can say Jack Robinson is an 18th-century phrase meaning immediately, or very quickly, and is said to refer to an erratic gentleman of that name who rushed around to visit his neighbours, rang the front-door bell, and then changed his mind and dashed off before the servant had time to announce his name.

All roads lead to Rome When Chaucer was writing of the 'astrolabe' (an ancient navigational instrument) during the late 14th century, he observed that 'diverse pathes leden diverse folk the righte way to Rome'.

The Romans gave us many things, amongst them the foundations for our legal, banking, and public postal systems, also our calendar, alphabet, and around one-third of the words in the English language. They left great buildings, aquaducts and canals, and a network of roads which radiated from the capital city of Rome across Europe to every part of the Empire. This last fact led to the general observation, including that of Chaucer, that on whichever road one started a journey it would, if one continued along it, eventually lead one to Rome.

In general conversation 'all roads lead to Rome' implies that sometimes any idea, or method of achieving an objective may be as good as any other since the result will, inevitably, be the same.

When in Rome, do as the Romans do comes from advice given by St Ambrose to St Augustine, which translated from the Latin reads: 'When in Rome, live as the Romans do; when elsewhere, live as they live elsewhere'. The statement is just as appropriate today as when it was first made almost 1,600 years ago. The suggestion is that when away from home one should adjust oneself and one's behaviour to the new surroundings and local customs, and not expect other people to alter their ways to yours.

Rome was not built in a day can be used in two ways — as encouragement to the faint-hearted not to give up, no matter how great the task or impossible the difficulties may seem, or as an excuse for delay in completing some job.

The historic city of ancient Rome, founded in 753 BC, became a wonder of the world with its magnificent buildings, architecture, palaces, temples, theatres, baths, aqueducts, bridges, seven hills, and glorious monuments. Such achievements take time, patience, and perseverance, and have served through the ages as a reminder that major works cannot be accomplished properly if done too hastily, whereas gradual, continuous, and determined efforts can achieve miracles.

Told sub rosa Anything told 'sub rosa' ('under the rose') is spoken in the strictest confidence and must not be repeated. The rose in question is the white rose which has for long been the emblem of silence. Whenever a white rose was hung above the banqueting table, no matter what was said or whatever the company, no secrets revealed were ever to be repeated. The custom originated with the Romans and spread to England, where it was widely used during the days of chivalry. It persisted until Victorian times when the living rose was replaced by a plaster motif carved in the ceilings of dining-rooms, many of which can still be seen today.

A bed of roses Few, if any, flowers are more popular than roses. Throughout their long history they have been used in every conceivable way — crowns of roses were placed on heads, rose petals were thrown at couples after marriage ceremonies, they were depicted on paintings carved and sculpted, made into perfume, and used to carpet floors at banquets during ancient Roman times. There were many other uses, including filling mattresses with rose petals.

Both Christopher Marlowe and William Shakespeare, born in the same year, 1564, mention the rose many times in their works. Marlowe, specifically refers to 'beds of roses'. If anyone is said to be on 'a bed of roses' they are in an extremely favourable situation experiencing pleasure and happiness.

Just as there is no rose without a thorn, however, pleasures are often fleeting and a 'bed of thorns', of course, implies the opposite meaning, expressing an extremely unpleasant situation or state of affairs, and the thorn is associated with disadvantages or sources of annoyance.

The three Rs refers to what have for long been considered the most important subjects pupils should be taught at school — reading, writing and arithmetic. The phrase may originate from a toast said to have been given by a former alderman and Lord Mayor of London, who could have benefited from a more thorough education himself. He raised his glass and said: 'To Reading, Riting and Rithmetic'.

Officers serving in the Navy under Admiral Fisher (1841–1920) learned of three more Rs. Fisher expected them to honour the code and be ruthless, relentless, and remorseless; he also advised them to 'never explain and never to apologize'.

There's the rub This phrase is used in the famous 'To be, or not to be' — soliloquy in Shakespeare's *Hamlet*, in the lines:

> To die, to sleep;
> To sleep, perchance to dream. Ay there's the rub;
> For in that sleep of death what dreams may come
> When we have shuffled off this mortal coil?

The 'rub' refers to the point at which some doubt, or difficulty, arises to cause a problem. Sir Francis Drake must have been well acquainted with the word, for it was used in the ancient game of bowls to describe anything which hindered the free movement of the 'wood', whether it be a slight undulation in the turf or a wood being diverted by an opponent's bowl. Hence the proverb: 'Those who play at bowls must look for rubbers'.

To cross the Rubicon means to make a decision, or take a course of action, or decisive step, which once embarked upon cannot be altered, and from which there can be no turning back or opportunity to change one's mind. The phrase arose from the action of Julius Caesar, in 49 BC, when he was ordered to disband his army. Instead of doing so he led his dedicated legion across the shallow river Rubicon, which bounded his

Gallic province in northern Italy, and marched against Rome, exclaiming 'the die is cast'. This brought about what amounted to a declaration of war against the Senate.

Fortunately for Caesar, his decision was successful and he became master of the Roman world.

To run for your life is to get away from danger or difficulty as fast as you can, but the likely origin of this advice does not necessarily offer any guarantee of success. For when one of the Duke of Monmouth's men, a noted fast runner, was captured after the Battle of Sedgemoor, in 1685, he was informed that his life would be spared if he could out-run a horse.

With no alternative offered (*see* 'Hobson's Choice') he was roped beside a stallion which was then let loose to race across the Somerset countryside. Although he kept pace with the horse, and it became exhausted before he did, those who had offered him this chance to save his life broke their promise and hanged him.

Not worth a rush In medieval times, fragrant herbs, rushes and leaves were used for strewing on the floors to freshen the apartments. As rank and social status was of more importance than it is today, it is possible that the rooms of some visitors or guests were 'not worth a rush', though this explanation for the phrase seems unlikely.

Rushes were also used for lighting, and it seems more plausible to suppose that guests who were not considered of sufficient importance to be given one were 'not worth a rush', particularly when the later expression of 'not worth a light' is considered. Alternatively, it could have referred to people in their own homes who got so used to undressing and going to bed in the dark that they didn't bother with a rush-light. The rushes used for illumination were more refined than those for strewing; they were often featured in household accounts of the time and had to be used economically.

To get the sack is to be dismissed from one's job. It is said to have originated from the days when workmen carried the tools of their trade and belongings in a bag, or sack, which they lodged with their employer.

When they were discharged, their employer gave them the sack back and sent them on their way to find another job elsewhere. The phrase is still widely used, although 'to get one's cards' has been a common alternative since National Insurance cards were introduced in Britain, in 1911.

Sail *see* To sail under FALSE colours

Salad days Shakespeare mentions these in *Antony & Cleopatra* (Act 1, Scene 5): 'My salad days, when I was green in judgement'. The reference is to the years of inexperienced youth — green is the fresh colour of young vegetables used in salads, and represents anyone who is young and lacking in experience. This also accounts for the use of the terms 'green' and 'greenhorn' for anyone considered to be a novice, raw hand, or simpleton.

An aunt Sally refers to anyone in the unhappy position of being the target for ridicule, or the person towards whom others can express their annoyance or anger. The original aunt Sally was a wooden model of a woman's head (mounted on a pole) with a pipe in the mouth, at which the public threw sticks or balls in a game at fairs. The object was to break the pipe or knock the head off the pole. The phrase is often used today to apply to anyone (of either sex) who is having to take all the knocks and is thus being treated unfairly.

Above the salt In the houses of important people, and the well-to-do, it was the custom to place the salt in its large silver container, in the middle of the long dining-table. Guests of honour were seated between the container and the head of the table, with those of less importance below it. Hence the expression to 'sit above (or below) the salt'.

Salt has since biblical times been esteemed as the emblem of eternity and immortal life — because of its ability to preserve things from decay. It has also been used as a protection against the forces of evil.

Even to this day, to spill salt is considered to be unlucky. Tradition has it that it must not be cleared up until a little has been thrown three times over the left shoulder with the right hand. If this is done, misfortune will be averted.

Not worth his salt Before money was introduced, the soldiers and workers in ancient Roman times had their wages paid in salt. When it is said of someone that he is 'not worth his salt' it means that he is not worth his wages, or not pulling his weight.

Alternatively, anyone referred to as 'the salt of the earth' means that they are dependable, honest, of excellent character, and hard working.

To be made a scapegoat refers to anyone who takes the blame and suffers for the misdeeds of others. It is mentioned in the Old Testament (Leviticus 16: 10) when on the Day of Atonement a goat was chosen by lot to bear the sins of the people, and then led into the wilderness and turned loose to 'carry' those sins away.

Schemes *see* The best laid schemes of mice and MEN

Scot free 'Scot' was the old name for payment, corresponding to modern tax, levied according to a person's ability to pay. To 'get off scot free' in earlier times meant that a person did not have to pay anything. Today, it is still used to describe anyone who has been let off payment, and can also refer to a person who has escaped from a tricky situation unpunished, or unharmed, and is safe.

To come up to scratch is to do what is expected of one, and not shirk one's duties.

In the days of bare-fisted boxing matches, before there was a proper ring, contestants had to toe a line scratched on the ground between them, or 'come up to scratch', before the fight could start.

Competitors in races also had to 'come up to scratch' — the line marked out, or scratched, from which the race would commence.

To start 'from scratch' means to start a race, game, or undertaking from the beginning, without any advantages or help, while 'to scratch' a horse or competitor's name from a race means that they will not be 'coming up to scratch', as they have been withdrawn.

[126]

To screw oneself up to concert pitch is to summon up one's courage, or state of readiness and fitness for a job or performance, to the highest degree. The pitch of any note depends on the number of vibrations per second which reach the ear-drum: the more vibrations per second, the higher the pitch of the note. When members of an orchestra tune their instruments for a concert, they often do so slightly higher than the normal pitch.

A higher pitch is obtained on stringed instruments by increasing the tension of the string, by turning or 'screwing up' the pegs. While kettle-drums (timpani), which are the only drums which can produce notes of a definite pitch, have 'screws' or 'taps' for adjusting the tension.

Seal of approval In the days when many people could neither read nor write, seals were put on the documents of various transactions as proof that they were authentic. The original seals used by the ancient Sumerians, 5,000 years ago, were made from precious and semi-precious stones which had engraved figures on them. The stones were cylindrical and when they were rolled over the soft clay of the writing tablets they left the impression of the seal, used by its owner.

Seals have been used of lead, but by medieval times those used on documents were made of wax. Sometimes large numbers of people were involved in an agreement — some of the documents in Britain's Public Record Office have fifty different seals, others almost 100, either on the documents themselves and/or hanging from them.

In more recent times any document 'given under hand and seal' indicated that it had been signed and sealed, and therefore approved of and confirmed by that person. Signet-rings, with seals set in them, were used instead of, or with, a signature as authentication. Later still, seals secured envelopes so that the contents might remain confidential between the sender and the receiver.

What did your last servant die of? comes to us from the days when even relatively small households of modest means had servants. A typical day in the life of a maid involved rising at 6 am, or earlier, and washing in cold water. Then, after dressing in her uniform, she would have to clean out the kitchen grate, black-lead it, and relight the fire as well as all the others in the house. She would have to clean and often polish the front doorstep. Next she laid the table for breakfast and continued to wait on her master, mistress and family during all meals throughout the day, as well as cleaning and washing up afterwards. In short, this was slaving sixteen hours a day, with possibly half a day off a month, for a few shillings a week . . . with deductions for any breakages!

Faced with such restrictions and an almost intolerable workload, it is hardly surprising that servants slumped, into bed exhausted in the evenings. Nor is it surprising that the question 'What did your last servant die of?' should have become popular as a retort to anyone who keeps asking someone to do one thing after another or, more accurately, one thing too much, when they are perfectly capable of, and should be, doing the job for themselves.

Shanks' pony To 'Go by Shanks' Pony' is to walk or go on foot, as opposed to riding.

Shank is an old-fashioned word for leg, in common use at the time of Edward I, who was one of the greatest kings ever to occupy the English throne, as well as being exceptionally tall for those times, and remembered affectionately by the name of 'Longshanks'.

Shakespeare refers to the shank, that part of the leg between the knee and ankle, in *As You Like It*, (2. 7), in the speech about the seven ages of man:

> The sixth age shifts into the lean and slipper'd pantaloon,
> With spectacles on nose and pouch on side,
> His youthful hose, well sav'd, a world too wide —
> For his shrunk shank . . .

Shank, in fact, is a very old word; reference is made to it in one of Aesop's fables. A stag drinking from the bank of a clear stream saw his image in the water, and contemplated it. 'Well' said he, 'if these Pitiful Shanks of mine were but answerable to this Branching Head, I can but think how I should defy all my enemies.'

The moment he said this, a pack of dogs came in full cry towards him. He immediately took flight, hastening across the fields to make for a wood but, as he went through a thicket, his horns became trapped in the bushes holding him fast until the hounds arrived and plucked him down. As he uttered his last words he said, 'What an unhappy fool was I, to take my friends for my enemies, and my enemies for my friends! I trusted to my *Head*, that has betray'd me, and I found fault with my *Legs*, that would otherwise have brought me off.'

Shape up or ship out means to smarten up, get on with the job, and improve one's performance. The phrase was used in World War II and has been carried over today into civilian life, but probably arose many centuries ago from the port of Bristol's world-wide reputation for good order and efficiency. (*See* SHIP-SHAPE and Bristol fashion').

Shape *see* To LICK into shape

A close shave is experienced by anyone who has had a narrow escape, a near miss, or has survived some ordeal, possibly of an adventurous nature. The phrase also may be used when success is narrowly achieved in the face of almost inevitable failure.

According to an early 17th-century proverb, 'barbers first learn to shave, by shaving fools'. No doubt victims experienced many 'a close shave' during the process. Later, in the 18th century, there were further hazards as heads were also shaved for the fashionable wigs. The barbers also acted as surgeons, and the ancient practice of bleeding a patient was still commonly attempted as a remedy for almost any ailment.

A spirally painted pole, of red and white stripes, was used as a sign outside barbers' shops. The pole represented the staff gripped by the patient as the vein was cut, and its red stripes represented the blood, and the white spiral the bandage needed.

During Charles II's reign (1660–1685), medicine and surgery became established as important sciences. By 1745, the Company of Barber Surgeons, which dated from 1462, was dissolved, and the trade of barber was separated from that of surgeon. Nevertheless, in the mid-eighteenth century, anaesthetics and the causes of infection were still unknown and surgery was hazardous, so it was only used as a last resort.

Black sheep The 'black sheep' of the family is a bad person or scoundrel who brings disgrace to the family. A saying, of 19th-century origin, 'there are black sheep in every flock' suggests that there is a scoundrel in every family, group, or community. Shepherds are said to dislike black sheep, and such a character in their flock could well be termed their *bête noir* (French for 'black beast').

Wild sheep were first domesticated by man at least 9,000 years ago. Today, they are only to be found in mountainous regions of the world. The Bighorn sheep of North America is one of the largest varieties of wild sheep, the massive circling horns of the males accounting for their name. The original wild sheep were tamed for their meat, wool and milk, but although their coats were thick they were not woolly like those of domestic sheep.

The Soay sheep on the island of St Kilda, beyond the Outer Hebrides, off north-west Scotland, are the closest relatives to our prehistoric sheep and still survive there in their wild state. Soay sheep were used principally by

Iron Age man for their fine, soft, wool which — as there were no suitable tools — had to be plucked, not sheared, in the early summer. Soay wool varies in colour from oatmeal to dark brown and it is probable that patterns were woven into cloths, on simple looms, based on the natural colours. The practice still survives today in the northern isles. The dark wool of any black sheep in the flocks was probably welcomed in those times as it could have been used without the need for dyeing, and black was then probably regarded as a practical colour, just as it is nowadays.

Sheep *see* May as well be HANGED for a sheep as a lamb

All ship-shape and Bristol fashion is to have everything neat and tidy, well-organized, and in good order — and comes from the port of Bristol's reputation for efficiency.

The city of Bristol has always gained its livelihood as a trading centre and its inhabitants took a leading part in the early voyages of discovery. It was from Bristol, in 1497, that the Cabots sailed on their voyage, financed mainly by local merchants, to explore the New World discovered by Columbus. Bristol ships and seafarers carried supplies to the first English colonies in America, Virginia and Newfoundland. The city was also the home of Admiral Penn, father of the founder of Pennsylvania.

With such a background it is not surprising that Bristol — at one time the largest port in Britain — should have gained a reputation second to none for efficiency and, thus, given rise to this expression.

When my ship comes home refers to the days when the merchant traders waited for their ships to return laden with goods, which they hoped to sell at considerable profit, and thus make them rich. The phrase, when used today, no longer refers literally to ships, but to any circumstance that will suddenly provide one with a fortune. When this happens it will be a time to rejoice, or pay debts, or both. But, more often than not, the phrase is used when there is little chance of this happening.

Ship *see* SHAPE up or ship out

Ship *see* To spoil the ship for a hap'orth 'o TAR

On a shoestring Many projects have to be done 'on a shoestring', or 'within a shoestring budget', i.e. with very little money. The phrase, which came into being through comparing the thinness of a shoelace

[130]

with the smallness of an amount of money, is of comparatively recent origin. The scandal was the earliest form of footwear worn by man, fastened by thongs which were sometimes brought up and bound round the ankle. Greek boots, however, were often fastened with criss-cross lacing. The boot- or shoe-lace as we know it did not come into wide use until the first half of the 19th century when the factory system of manufacture and machinery made it possible to turn out a pair of boots or shoes within minutes, instead of the whole day required when the work was done by hand.

To shoot one's bolt This phrase is based on the old proverb 'a fool's bolt is soon shot' — the bolt was the short, heavy arrow used in a crossbow. A foolish archer, therefore, was someone who shot all his bolts too soon, leaving none in reserve. When used in everyday speech the phrase means that one has used up all one's resources, or made one's final effort too soon, perhaps by speaking up prematurely and being quickly silenced.

(*See* 'no SHOT in one's locker'.)

No shot in one's locker indicates that all one's resources are spent. The phrase comes from the days of the sailing warship. The ammunition was kept in lockers and when the lockers were empty the ship could no longer fight and carry out its main function. The nautical phrase was later taken up on shore to imply that the speaker was hard up and had no money in his pocket. (*See* 'to SHOOT one's bolt'.)

To give short shrift to anyone today means to deal with them swiftly and curtly, and generally to treat them in an unsympathetic manner.

In the Middle Ages when justice was harsh, and executions frequent, a condemned man would barely be given a chance to say anything before sentence of hanging was passed.

Later, in the 16th century, when 'short shrift' was introduced it came to mean the short time, of a few minutes, allowed before the execution of a criminal, during which he was allowed to make his confession to a priest and be granted absolution for his sins.

Sit *see* To sit on the FENCE

At sixes and sevens refers to a general state of confusion, or to a situation in which an agreement or decision seems impossible, and has yet to be made.

[131]

The expression is said to have originated from the rivalry between the craftsmen's guilds, which were established in the Middle Ages in Britain and Europe to look after their interests. A large number of trades were represented — weavers, goldsmiths, dyers, glove-makers, saddlers and shoemakers — and great rivalry existed between them. A dispute arose between two of the guilds within the City of London — the Merchant Taylors, and the Skinners — as to which should be sixth in order of precedence, and which seventh. When the Lord Mayor intervened, he resolved the situation, by suggesting that the two companies should take it in turns to be ranked sixth and seventh.

Skeleton at the feast Many families have a 'skeleton in the cupboard', i.e. a family secret, a discreditable or humiliating fact that they wish to keep concealed from strangers. But a 'skeleton at the feast' has an entirely different meaning, based on the ancient Egyptian custom of placing a skeleton in a seat at their banquets to remind everyone of their mortal state. Today, the expression is used to describe someone, or something, that spoils the general enjoyment at a dinner party or other festive occasion.

Sleep on a clothes line In the 19th century life was exceptionally tough for the poor in cities. Many of those who could not afford a bed, nor face the workhouse, slept on what was known as the 'twopenny rope'. This was the sum charged to allow men to sit on a bench and lean on a line stretched taut in front of them for the night. In the morning the 'sleepers' were awoken abruptly by the landlord cutting the rope to send them on their way. Today, when people are exhausted they often say, 'I'm so tired I could sleep on a clothes' line'.

In London then it was said that every night 'a 100,000 men knew not where they would lay their heads'. Anyone lucky enough to find a lodging house could expect to find an open sewer running under the floor, while those not fortunate enough to be able to afford to pay for such luxury were lucky if they could find overnight shelter in casual wards, which were nothing more than stables without straw or bedding. Those admitted to the workhouse were turned away without bread in the morning, unless they first broke stones in the yard. Anyone willing to do this, the officials reasoned, must surely be destitute, and not a malingerer.

A Harvey Smith is a gesture used to denote contempt. One of Britain's most brilliant sportsmen, Harvey Smith, the internationally famous show-jumper, was alleged to have raised two fingers at Mr Douglas Bunn, one of the judges, and originator of Hickstead, after completing the winning round of the Sussex course, at the August 1971 meeting. The course was difficult, competition keen, and the reward relatively high but, because of his action, Harvey Smith was informed that the prize money would be withheld. After consultations and deliberations, he was exonerated some while later and awarded the prize money.

Although Harvey Smith's name has remained associated with it, the gesture was by no means new, having been used widely during the 1930s. It also found its way into an RAF pilot's log book in an entry dated 1 July, 1941 after flying his slow aircraft into a strong headwind: 'Given rude two-fingered gesture from motorcyclist, overtaking below'.

To hit a snag No one can go through life without coming across some snag or another. Originally, a 'snag' was an old Scandinavian word for a spike, or any jagged projecting point, such as the broken branch of a tree, or the pointed stump sticking out of the ground. 'To hit a snag' is to come up against some unexpected difficulty or obstruction in one's progress or plans. (*See* 'the best laid schemes of MICE and MEN'.)

Soapbox *see* To get off one's HOBBY HORSE

Put a sock in it When Thomas Edison, the American inventor, produced his phonograph, in 1877, it captured the first sound ever to be recorded — a recitation of 'Mary had a little lamb' which could be preserved and reproduced time and again. Some ten years later another inventor, Emil Berliner, produced the first gramophone to play disc records. The turntable was originally rotated by hand, then by the spring of a motor wound up by hand. The sounds of speech, music and song emerged through a large horn, and much later from a resonance box, both of which greatly magnified the sound.

One thing which was lacking on many machines, however, despite other technical advances, was any form of volume control. Many a teenager, or adult, was told to 'put a sock in it', which meant, literally, doing just that. A woollen sock was placed inside the horn, or resonance box, to reduce the offending noise. If the record was a particulrly loud one, many socks were needed. Gramophones were still having socks thrust into them in the 1920s and even in the 1930s, in some cases, before all machines were fitted with the necessary volume controls.

Anyone today playing a stereo record player with the volume turned too high for the comfort of others is often still told to 'put a sock in it'. The expression is still used in its more general and humorous sense to stop someone talking too much.

Sod's law Most people have heard of Boyle's law, Ohm's law, or the law of gravity. In more recent times a new law has come into the vocabulary which affects every one of us — 'Sod's Law'. This is a modern slang expression used in everyday life, commerce and industry, to imply that if anything can go wrong with any plan, idea, or activity . . . it will!

Something old, something new; something borrowed, something blue is a saying associated with the blessing of marriages, to ensure good fortune, which has been used for centuries by almost everyone, whether they are superstitious or not.

'A woman seldom asks advice until she has bought her wedding clothes'. So wrote Joseph Addison, the English poet, essayist and shrewd observer of human nature, in an issue of *The Spectator*, in 1712. But one piece of advice which few brides choose to ignore is to wear 'something old, something new, something borrowed, and something blue' in their wedding outfit.

Ahead lies an entirely new life, calling for clothing which is also entirely new. A white dress is considered lucky, and some accessory of blue is included to make even more certain of good luck. Originally, 'something old' usually meant the shoes. Alternatively, it could be the veil, handed down through the generations. 'Something borrowed' could be anything, even a safety-pin, or lump of sugar, which some brides still carry in their wedding gloves to bring 'sweetness to their married lives'. If the bride also carried a coin, old or new, it was believed to secure future wealth.

'Blue' was also used in the 'bride-favours' of the 17th century, consisting of knots of ribbons stitched loosely on to the wedding gown, which could be snatched off by young men at the wedding feasts. The carnation or other flower buttonholes, worn today by male guests at weddings are a relic of the old luck-bringing bride-favours. The 'something blue', so far as the bride is concerned today, often takes the form of a garter.

If none of these customs, devices, and old traditions worked in bringing good luck and fortune to a marriage, and a wife subsequently became unfaithful to her husband, it was *he* who was ridiculed and had to face the gossip, with the added humiliation of being called 'cuckold'. A word derived from cuckoo, the bird that lays its eggs in another's nest.

[134]

Son of a gun was used originally as an expression of contempt but, subsequently, took the form of a light-hearted greeting. Its popularity was at its height in the 1930s and through World War II. It was usually addressed to someone who had done something unusual, that he perhaps should not have done, yet had got away with it, and could only be admired for his audacity.

The original meaning of the phrase arose in the days when women were sometimes allowed to accompany men in ships of the Navy. (*See* 'show a LEG'.) Voyages were frequently long, and conditions cramped, and any woman about to give birth had to do so beneath, or beside, one of the ship's guns, behind an improvised screen.

Captain of one's soul When someone is dominated by another person, it is often said of them that they cannot even call their soul their own. To be 'the captain of one's soul' refers to the happier state of affairs where a person is in full control of their present circumstances, and any events likely to face them in the future. The phrase was made famous by William Ernest Henley, the British 19th-century poet and dramatist, in his poem *Invictus*:

> I am the master of my fate:
> I am the captain of my soul.

Sour *see* Sour GRAPES

In a flat spin Anyone in these circumstances is liable to be in a confused state of mind, and so busy that they are rushing around and getting nowhere. They may be petrified and even panic-stricken.

The phrase came into widespread use between the wars, in the days when test pilots frequently went off on what were 'one way trips' — taking off in an aeroplane, and returning by parachute after a mid-air break up, or malfunction of some vital part. This happened particularly when testing prototypes, or the first new machines of any new type of aircraft. Amongst the tests that had to be carried out were spinning trials. In many instances, newly-designed aircraft became locked in spins and the pilot would be unable to recover control. The worst type of spin was known as a 'flat spin', in which the nose went high and the aeroplane spun flatly, instead of spirally and nose-down, around its vertical axis. Some of the aircraft, which were sound in every other way, had to be fitted with anti-spin devices, such as a small parachute attached to the tail which was released by the pilot to arrest the aeroplane's speed or attitude, to bring it out of the spin.

During the mid 1930s one married couple owed their lives to a flat spin. They were flying together over southern England in a low-winged private aeroplane when, suddenly, the propeller-driven engine parted company with the fuselage and shot out of the nose. The husband was at the controls in the rear open cockpit, and his wife in front of him was virtually sitting 'in space'. The aeroplane went into a spin . . . then, after a few seconds, into the dreaded 'flat spin' from which they could not recover. Neither had a parachute. They gyrated in this fashion towards the earth, crashed, but then stepped out unharmed. If the aeroplane had spun normally, nose downwards, they would have been killed. In its 'flat spin' the aircraft had struck the ground in a horizontal position, while still rotating in the manner of a flat stone thrown to skim over water, with the minimum impact.

Spoil *see* To spoil the ship for a hap'orth 'o TAR

Born with a silver spoon in one's mouth At one time it was customary for godparents to give a silver spoon to their godchildren at christenings. Although such children were invariably born of rich parents, and liable to inherit wealth and fortune from birth, the silver spoon was welcome and it would have been considered bad taste for godparents to have given anything less. Sometimes a silver apostle spoon was given; a particularly lucky child might be presented with a complete set of twelve spoons bearing the figure of an apostle at the top of each handle.

The phrase is used, today, to describe anyone born of rich parents, and also, more generally, applied to anyone who always appears lucky, and seems to be successful whatever they do.

Anyone who has a set of apostle spoons, dating from the 16th or 17th centuries, can be considered lucky, even if they were not born of rich parents. Complete sets in good condition are rare and fetch high prices when offered at auction. One such set from Elizabethan times at Christie's, London, was sold for £70,000 in 1974.

Up the spout is a phrase used to describe anyone in a desperate plight, particularly a financial one, and comes from the 'spout' (lift) which was used in pawnbrokers' shops. When articles were pledged in exchange for cash they were sent 'up the spout' to the storeroom where they remained until their owner could afford to redeem them. Then, when the loan and interest were repaid, they were returned down the spout. The description also came to be applied, quite often, to mechanical objects which were said to be 'up the spout' when they wouldn't work, or were out of commission.

To spruce up is to smarten oneself up, in one's dress, appearance, and behaviour. The phrase comes from Prussia with its reputation for military smartness. The spruce tree is both elegant and neat, and actually takes its name from an early spelling of Prussia.

Spruce trees have a life-span of around 150 years and can reach a similar height in feet (over 45 metres). The most familiar species is the Norwegian spruce, used in Europe as a Christmas tree. The custom of decorating it and making it look even more attractive was introduced into Britain from Germany in 1844, during Queen Victoria's reign, by Prince Albert.

To win one's spurs is to prove oneself, and gain recognition and distinction.

When a man was knighted in medieval times he was given a pair of gilt spurs in honour of his chivalry. The honour was not given lightly and was only awarded after a long term of apprenticeship, started when a boy of noble birth reached the age of twelve or so. A long thorough training in courtly ways, and the management of horses and weapons was given. The first goal was becoming a squire and receiving a pair of silver spurs. If his progress continued to be satisfactory, he would begin fighting in battles when aged seventeen. Distinction and valour in the field could lead to the gilded, or golden spurs of knighthood.

One of the most celebrated heroes of English chivalry was the Black Prince, elder son of Edward III, who was given command of a wing of the English forces when he was only sixteen years old at the Battle of Crécy in 1346. Although his army was outnumbered by four to one, he led his men into action and victory with great skill and daring, and won his spurs in the battle.

He was involved in several more battles and achieved an even greater victory ten years later at the Battle of Poitiers, in which he captured the French king himself.

Fate dictated that the Black Prince, who later became the Prince of Wales, should never rule the kingdom for which he fought so well and whose interests were so close to his heart. He died, aged forty-six, a year before his father.

Let off steam *see* To BLOW one's top

[137]

On the stocks refers to something that is in hand, but not yet completed. The phrase comes from the wooden frame, or 'stocks', in which a ship is placed while being built. So long as it is there it is said to be 'on the stocks', in other words, in the course of construction.

During the days of Nelson a stout oaken vessel of 1,300 tons required the felling of more than 2,000 average oak trees. The oldest of the great English forests, inappropriately named the New Forest, in Hampshire, for long provided the bulk of the timber for the Navy. During the 18th century, the New Forest possessed its own flourishing shipbuilding yards, notably at the little village of Buckler's Hard on the west bank of the Beaulieu River. No fewer than sixty-seven vessels were built from merchant-men to man-of-war, including three ships which fought at Trafalgar: the 36-gun *Euryalus*, 74-gun *Swiftsure*, and Nelson's favourite ship the 64-gun *Agamemnon*.

The launching of each ship was a big occasion, often attracting as many as 10,000 spectators, George III and Queen Charlotte attended when the 74-gun *Illustrious* was launched in 1789.

The genius behind all this enterprise was the master-builder, Henry Adams. He was succeeded by his son Robert. When Edward and Balthasar Adams followed him they made the mistake of over-reaching themselves by having four men-of-war 'on the stocks' at the same time. It was an impossible task and when they were unable to fulfil their contract, the Admiralty imposed a catastrophic fine which they were unable to meet, and this resulted in the ship-yard having to be closed.

Stools *see* FALL between two stools

To pull out all the stops is to put all one's efforts and energies into something in order to achieve an objective. The phrase refers to the organ player who performs an almost superhuman task in manipulating numerous 'stops' to achieve the effects required, while using both hands and both feet independently, and playing on several keyboards at once. Some organs have hundreds of stops which connect groups of pipes to the keyboard and modify the sound produced. Multiple console models have well over a thousand. If all the stops were pulled out, the organist would be achieving a maximum performance, but the volume would be intolerable, and probably sufficient to bring any building, particularly an ancient one, tumbling down.

The instrument originated in ancient Greece as Pan Pipes. By the third century BC the Romans had invented the 'Hydraulus' in which air was forced into the pipes by water-power. Centuries later, this was achieved by bellows. The early organs were used during public entertainments and it was not until the middle of the fifth century AD that they were introduced into the church, first in Spain and then, some two centuries later, in Rome.

Portable or 'portative' organs were still used widely in England during the Middle Ages in processions as well as in chamber music. When the organ became a static instrument and important in its own right, refinements were added to its construction and performance until it came to be regarded as the 'king of instruments'. Most organs have pipes which imitate the sounds of other instruments, operated by pulling out the required 'stops'.

Two composers who probably pulled out all the stops in their time, putting everything into their performances, were Bach and Handel. Both came from Germany, both were superlative organists, and both suffered blindness in old age.

Any port in a storm dates from the 18th century. The phrase is used to suggest that when one is faced with difficulties or danger any refuge, or offer of help, is welcome, even though it may mean sinking one's pride and accepting assistance from a person or place one dislikes.

Stormy *see* A stormy PETREL

Making bricks without straw Without straw, of course, bricks will crack and fall to pieces. When anyone says 'you cannot make bricks without straw', he is stating that nothing can be achieved without the necessary materials, whether these be adequate tools, special facilities, or sufficient capital resources to launch and maintain a project.

The phrase originated in Biblical times, and is to be found in *Exodus*. Bricks were then made of mud, mixed with chopped straw to prevent them from shrinking and cracking as they dried. If slaves were ordered by a cruel taskmaster to 'make bricks without straw', life was made even harder as their task was almost impossible. If they were expected to make the same number of bricks each day without straw, that meant making twice as many bricks to allow for failures, as only the good bricks were counted.

The last straw When things continue to go wrong, and one difficulty follows another, we do our best to cope. But, very often, there is one trouble too many, something quite small in itself but which, coupled to

[139]

all the other problems, proves to be 'the last straw' and too much for us to take.

The phrase, which goes back to the 17th century, refers to the supposition that if a camel's load is increased straw by straw the stage will be reached where the addition of one final straw will be enough to 'break the camel's back'.

A man of straw is someone who has no scruples and is prepared to do anything for gain.

Outside courts in the past, it was common for men who were willing to give false evidence for money to parade with a straw in one of their shoes. The straw signalled that they were ready to swear to anything for the appropriate fee.

Lightning strike 'A lightning strike' is widely used today to describe a withdrawal of labour at short notice. The word 'strike' originated in the mid-18th century in the days of sail when seamen with a grievance refused to sail, and 'struck' (lowered) the sails and yards of the ship to prevent it from embarking on its voyage.

> 'Here lies a man who was killed by lightning;
> He died when his prospects seemed to be brightening.
> He might have cut a flash in this world of trouble,
> But the flash cut him, and he lies in the stubble'.

They say that 'lightning never strikes twice'. The above anonymous epitaph for the unfortunate gentleman of Great Torrington, in Devon, shows that once is enough. However, many people have, in fact, been struck by lightning on more than one occasion in various parts of the world: Roy Sullivan of Virginia in the USA was struck on no less than seven occasions, and survived.

Lightning is still terrifying to most people, particularly when it is close, and it must have been even more terrifying to our ancestors, who knew nothing of science or meteorology, and could only put it down to the wrath of the gods, or the work of evil spirits. This is why, for centuries, certain trees and plants were believed to provide protection from this phenomenon. If a houseleek, for instance, grew on the roof of a house and was not disturbed, the belief was that the house would never be burnt down, or struck by lightning. Church bells were also rung during thunderstorms to prevent lightning damage to people, property and crops. The custom is still continued as a precaution in some European countries today.

There is, of course, every reason to fear lightning — the energy dissipated in one lightning strike is greater than the output of a large modern power station. Lightning consists of two flashes: the first flash, called the leader stroke, is caused by the negative charge in the cloud striking the positively charged ground, and the return second stroke flashes up from the ground, back along the same initial narrow path to the cloud, heating the air around it to a tremendously high temperature, which expands the air, causing thunder. The leader and return strokes happen so quickly that they appear as a single strike to the human eye. The return stroke travels at a much higher velocity — up to 87,000 miles/sec (140,000 km/sec), which is almost half the speed of light.

Any expressions with the words 'lightning' or 'like lightning' in them, therefore, mean with the greatest conceivable speed. The alternative phrase of going 'like the clappers', which also means very quickly, is more likely to be derived from the 'clap' of thunder associated with these storms, than from the clapper of a bell.

To pull strings — To have on a string The word 'string' is derived from the Anglo-Saxon *strang*, meaning strong. TO PULL STRINGS is to use one's influence behind the scenes to gain an advantage, by manipulating someone, or something. TO HAVE SOMEONE, OR SOMETHING, ON A STRING implies that one has control. Both phrases are associated with puppets, whose movements are manipulated and controlled through the use of strings.

A stumbling block *see* TO BALK someone

One swallow does not make a summer This saying, of ancient Greek origin, has its equivalent in many different countries. It serves as a reminder against the folly of reaching hasty conclusions, forming an opinion, or making a judgement on the basis of a single piece of evidence, when the safer and wiser thing to do is to wait for further proof.

Aristotle (384–322 BC), the Greek philosopher, amongst others through the centuries, did not believe swallows migrated in winter, but thought that they slept in holes in cliffs, or underground. Another theory, which was still current in England during the 16th and 17th centuries, held that swallows hibernated at the bottom of pools as they have the habit of swooping down to roost in the reeds on the edges of lakes and ponds at the approach of autumn. When observers went closer, the swallows had disappeared and were assumed to have hibernated. We know today that their sudden disappearance is accounted for by their migration to Africa, to winter south of the Sahara.

In the spring we are reminded that the return of one swallow does not make a summer — we have to wait, usually until May, when they have all returned.

Swan song is the last performance, or work produced by an actor, singer, or writer.

The false belief that swans sing melodiously just before they die, dates from ancient times. Both Plato and Aristotle mention it, and the expression is used by Shakespeare and many other poets. It has also been long held that the souls of the dead are embodied in swans. It was also believed that swans accompanied the dead to their last resting place.

The characteristics of the swan — the proud poise of the swan's graceful neck and its stately movements — seem to make it a favourite subject in literature, although Coleridge (1772–1834) had his own distinctive view on swan songs:

> Swans sing before they die — 'twere no bad thing
> Should certain persons die before they sing.

Sword *see* The sword of DAMOCLES

Sword *see* The PEN is mightier than the sword

All systems go means that all preparations and checks prior to action have been completed and everything is ready to start. The phrase has found its way into everyday use but was originated by American controllers during the launching of their rocket systems for the exploration of space.

The rocket launch was preceded by the 'count down', in which controllers counted the minutes and seconds, in decreasing numbers, until 'zero' was reached, when the motors were fired, and the rocket had 'lift-off'.

Space rockets, shuttles which can be re-used, and man-made satellites for space communication, or weather observation, have all become common, but the most remarkable space flight was the first landing on the moon by the American astronauts, in 1969. Neil Armstrong became the first man to set foot on the moon, and was seen and heard live by millions of television viewers all over the world. Armstrong's historic words on that July morning were: 'That's one small step for man, one giant leap for mankind.'

Old wives' tales

> 'Some folks are wise, and some are otherwise'.
>
> *Tobias Smollett*
> (1721–1771)

Old wives' tales are supposed to be unconvincing stories handed down from generation to generation, often from uneducated old women, which are foolish and based on old-fashioned ideas and accounts which are untrustworthy, even though they were believed to be true at the time.

Before we dismiss them we should, perhaps, heed the words of Edgar Allan Poe (1809–1849), the American poet, writer, and critic: 'It is the nature of truth in general, as of some ores in particular, to be richest when most superficial'. For amongst many of the old wives' tales there are nuggets of valuable information which can teach us much and enable us to profit from what we learn. Technology cannot solve everything and, as Tennyson observed, 'Knowledge comes, but wisdom lingers'. And Chaucer, some five centuries before him, when he asked: 'What is bettre than wisdom? Womman. And what is bettre than a good womman? No-thing'.

We can take, or leave, these old wives' tales as we wish, much in the way that in the eighteenth century Frederick the Great of Prussia is attributed with saying: 'My people and I have come to an agreement which satisfies us both. They are to say what they please, and I am to do what I please'.

Talk *see* To talk GIBBERISH

Talk *see* To TALK TURKEY

Talking *see* Talking through their HATS

To keep a tally The word 'tally' is derived from the Latin *talen*, a slip of wood which was scored with notches to mark transactions as a method of keeping accounts before most people could read or write. Seasoned willow or hazel sticks were generally used, and small notches indicated pence, larger notches shillings, and still larger ones pounds. The sticks were then split lengthwise, with the buyer and the seller each keeping one. If there was a dispute it could be settled by bringing the two halves together to see if they tallied.

Larger and wider notches were used to indicate £10, £50, £100 or as much as £1,000. Tallies were also used by the Exchequer of the English Government until the end of the 18th century, much in the way that Government Loan Certificates were issued later as documents of its indebtedness. A vast number of tallies accumulated during the course of 600 years, and when the Government ordered them to be disposed of in 1834, the stove used accidentally overheated and set fire to the old Houses of Parliament building.

We still 'keep a tally' on many things today, such as checking goods against invoices to make sure that they tally.

To spoil the ship for a hap'orth 'o tar is to risk ruining, or losing something valuable, through stupidity or failure to purchase some small item which can make all the difference between success and failure, or in achieving one's own, or a common, objective.

The *ship* does not refer to nautical vessels but to *sheep*, a word which, in many areas of England, is pronounced as 'ship'. To spoil the *sheep* for a hap'orth 'o tar originally meant losing a sheep by failing to protect its wounds or sores by treating them with the tar which was available at comparatively small cost and known to be effective.

Not my cup of tea — A storm in a teacup Tea drinking was first introduced into England in the 17th century and has remained popular with almost everyone ever since. The phrase NOT MY CUP OF TEA is used to imply that something is not to one's taste or not what one enjoys, or is suited for.

Tea drinking is associated with tranquility and the phrase A STORM IN A TEACUP, which originated in the 19th century, became the title of a farce by W. B. Bernard. Such a storm is an excitement or commotion over some trivial matter — or a fuss about nothing.

Crocodile tears The phrase 'crocodile tears' has been used not only in literature but in everyday speech for centuries. It means hypocritical grief and arose from the early belief that crocodiles wept while devouring their victims.

[144]

'It is the wisdom of the crocodiles, that shed tears when they would devour'. So observed Sir Francis Bacon (1561–1626). Crocodiles have been a favourite subject of poets and writers, including Edmund Spenser, Shakespeare and Lewis Carroll.

When crocodiles open their jaws wide, tears are shed automatically from their eyes — not from distress over devouring their prey, but from a natural reflex action. So any tears that are shed are insincere tears.

In its lifetime a crocodile sheds more tears than any other person or creature, for a crocodile is believed to live for two centuries or more.

No thanks, I'm teetotal is the sort of response made by anyone offered a drink who does not drink intoxicants, or declines after having 'signed the pledge' to abstain from them. The word 'teetotal' came into the language in 1833, immediately after a lecturer had advocated the temperance cause but stuttered as he did so and duplicated the letter 'T' of 'total' in saying, 'nothing but t-t-t-t-total abstinence will do . . .'.

Tell *see* To tell someone POINT blank

To be on tenterhooks is to be in a state of suspense, anxiety, or full of expectation. Fully stretched and under strain, in fact, as the word comes from the Latin 'tendre' meaning 'to stretch'.

The expression comes from cloth-making and weaving in which the finished material is stretched on a frame known as a 'tenter' with the cloth being attached to it at the edges by means of 'tenter hooks'.

At the end of one's tether is to be frustrated to such an extent that one has had enough; one's strength and patience are so exhausted that there is nothing more than one can do or bear. The 'tether' is the rope or chain which restricts grazing animals within a limited area.

To set the Thames on fire is to do something remarkable. The phrase is mostly used negatively to imply that a person, or an action, will not achieve anything important as in 'he will never set the Thames on fire'.

During Henry II's reign, work began on the new London Bridge over the river Thames, funded on money raised by a tax on wool. Some 500 years later, the closely-packed houses built on the bridge were set alight during the Great Fire of London. As the flaming parts of the buildings fell into the Thames, they, and the reflections, must have made the Thames almost look as though it were on fire. But the phrase is of later origin in the eighteenth century and comes from a misuse of the word 'Thames' which should have been *temse*, an old word for a corn-sieve. It was implied, as a joke, that an over-zealous labourer might work his 'temse' so hard that it could catch fire.

Throat *see* A FROG in the throat

To steal someone's thunder is to take the credit for someone else's achievement, work, or idea, or to anticipate their intended action and to put it into effect before them.

The phrase may have originated when a mid-17th century dramatist invented a machine for reproducing the sound of thunder to heighten the effect of one of his plays in the theatre. When he visited another theatre later he was dismayed to find that a rival had copied his idea and was using a similar machine. He proclaimed his displeasure by remarking that 'someone had stolen his thunder'.

That's the ticket In former times tickets were issued to the poor to exchange for the bare necessities of life, such as soup, clothing, and fuel. Nowadays it is more likely to apply to the winning ticket in a lottery. Either way, the phrase means it is exactly right, just what is needed.

Take time by the forelock 'Time is like a river made up of events which happen, and its current is strong; no sooner does anything appear than it is swept away, and another comes in its place, and will be swept away too'.

When Marcus Aurelius Antoninus (121–180 AD), the great Roman Emperor and Philosopher, wrote this in his *Meditations* he was echoing the thoughts of Virgil (70–19 BC), the inspired Roman poet, who wrote: *Sed fugit interea, fugit inreparabile tempus* — 'Time meanwhile flies, flies never to return'.

The Latin phrase *tempus fugit* is used frequently today for 'time flies', whenever we notice that time is passing sooner than we think. Both examples from the Romans remind us of the comparatively recent phrase that it we don't 'take time by the forelock', and act immediately, time will pass and we could let a chance slip by. The reference to the forelock comes from Old Father Time, depicted as a bald old man, except for a lock of hair growing just above his forehead. If we find ourselves behind him, time has passed and we have missed our opportunity. Whereas, if we act quickly, without a moment's delay, we can face him from the front and grasp him by the forelock.

Time *see* In the NICK of time

Time *see* A WHALE of a time

To drink a toast At one time a piece of toast was put into tankards to improve the flavour of the ale. To drink the toast was a good excuse for having the tankard replenished, no doubt. But the meaning of the phrase as we know it today, to drink someone's health, or to propose a toast in honour of someone, is alleged to go back to the time of Charles II.

In the elegant and fashionable city of Bath, in Somerset (now Avon), a beau observed a beautiful lady enjoying the famous public baths. He dipped a glass in the water, held it up for all to see, and drank her health. Whereupon, a reveller, who had been enjoying more real liquor than the natural mineral water, jumped into the bath and declared that he would have nothing to do with the liquor but would have the toast . . . in other words, the lady herself.

Topsy-turvy

'Do you know who made you?'
'Nobody, as I knows on,' said Topsy with a short laugh, 'I 'spect I grow'd. Don't think nobody never made me.'

Harriet Beecher Stowe
(1811–1896)

When we use this expression today to describe anything that is upside down, or in a state of chaos, some people imagine that it originated with the child 'Topsy', in the famous American authoress Mrs Stowe's story of *Uncle Tom's Cabin*, who was both mischievous and ignorant and appeared to be in a state of utter confusion. Though the description is appropriate, 'topsy-turvy' is said to belong to the early-16th century; 'top' was added to the word 'terve', in use at the time, which meant 'to topple or overturn'.

The expression was already in use in Mrs Stowe's time. When the railroad spread to America, to be greeted with dismay, it was described by one New York newspaper as '. . . a pestilential, topsy-turvy, harum-scarum whirligig . . . in which citizens would be flying about like comets — and liable to suffocation when a-gadding at speeds of 20 miles an hour (32 km/h).'

Touch *see* Wouldn't touch with a BARGE pole

Touch and go is used to describe risky circumstances, in which the outcome can go one way or the other. If used in the past tense it refers to a narrow escape.

The phrase is of nautical origin, and arose from instances where a ship might touch the bottom but be able to continue without stopping — having 'touched' but 'gone' on her way.

It was said in the early days of aviation that any landing was a good one if the pilot could walk away from it. A nautical sentiment in the mid-19th century had it that 'touch and go was good pilotage'.

Touch *see* Touch WOOD

Trail *see* To BLAZE a trail

Trees *see* MONEY doesn't grow on trees

T's *see* To do the I's and cross the T's

To talk turkey is to talk purposefully about profitable matters, and 'cold turkey' is a demand for the straight truth. In recent times, the word 'bread' has come to mean money, and to ask for, or discuss 'bread', is in effect to suggest that one comes to some arrangement over a payment, or fee, or that one gets down to 'talking turkey'. The origin is obscure but probably comes from the gobble-gobble noise turkeys make, and the chatter between two people discussing money.

To turn one's coat When battle uniforms were colourful, rather than camouflaged, it was easy to see which side soldiers belonged to. Soldiers of fortune, however, often changed sides when it looked as though the side they were supporting was going to lose the battle, or when the conditions appeared better, or more lucrative, on the other side. The lining of their coat was a different colour from the outside, so all that was necessary was to turn one's coat inside out.

A renegade, or 'turncoat', today, refers to anyone who changes their mind and deserts their party or principles, and joins the opposing side or point of view; or, alternatively, keeps changing their mind and loyalties.

Turn *see* To turn over a new LEAF

To turn the tables on someone is to reverse the position or situation in one's favour. Most explanations for the phrase refer to losers cheating in games, such as chess and draughts, in which the table or board was often reversed to gain advantage over their opponent. But this seems unlikely as any opponent wide-awake enough to have been in a winning position would immediately have noticed any such change.

The more likely, and certainly the earliest, explanation is that the common maple tree, was so highly-prized by the Romans that they gave an extravagant price for its timber to make their tables. If the Romans reproached their wives for extravagance in jewels etc, the ladies used to 'turn the tables' upon their husbands, that is remind them of what they spent upon their maplewood tables.

The weakest go to the wall This expression is today used to imply the survival of the fittest — the weak being pushed aside, or doing badly in competition. Originally it meant something quite different, referring to an act of courtesy, in the days of coaching and heavy horse traffic, in which gentlemen positioned their ladies close to the wall, for safety, in streets which had no pavements.

The roads then, as now, were highly dangerous places and the proportion of people who were seriously injured in road accidents in London in the 1880s was almost the same as it is today, but only half as many were killed in ratio to population compared with the present.

In the 1880s there were up to 500,000 private carriages and over 7,000 hansom cabs in regular use. It was the public's nightmare, and the dream of the gardener and horticulturist — ten million tons of horse droppings were cleaned up each year from English towns. So, positioning the ladies close to the wall was not only the safest place for them to walk, but also the cleanest.

The writing on the wall This phrase comes from the Bible (Daniel 5). A mysterious hand is seen writing on the wall during a feast given by King

[149]

Belshazzer. As the king watched the disembodied hand writing, his thoughts were troubled. None of the wise men called upon were able to interpret the words and the king became even more worried. When, finally, Daniel was summoned, he informed the king that the words foretold the downfall of his kingdom and the death of the king himself. That night, Belshazzer was slain.

Today the phrase is still used in its original sense, to serve as a warning of impending disaster.

Walls *see* Walls have EARS

Warts and all When Oliver Cromwell sat for his portrait he is said to have instructed Sir Peter Lely, the artist, to paint him as he saw him, 'warts and all'. The painter was famous for his portraits of beautiful women and Cromwell did not want him to waste his skills in flattery. Cromwell was aware that his nose was rather large and that there were one or two skin blemishes on his face. Although regarded otherwise by his enemies, he had a sense of humour and a lighter side to his character. What Cromwell actually said to Lely is recorded as: 'Remark all these roughnesses, pimples, warts, and everything as you see me, otherwise I will never pay a farthing for it'.

If anyone is asked to portray something, or someone, 'warts and all', this is a request for a true representation, showing the defects as well as the good points.

A whale of a time is a hugely enjoyable time. (The whale is the largest animal that has ever lived, dwarfing even the largest living mammal, the elephant.)

There are two kinds of whales: the whalebone whales and the toothed whales. The former includes the world's largest animal, the blue whale which grows to over 100 feet (30 m) long and over 150 tonnes in weight. A newborn calf weighs around 8 tonnes and is 25 feet (7 m) long, on average. Although they grow to such a vast size, blue whales eat some of the smallest animals in the sea — shrimp-like creatures called krill, and other minute sea food.

Wet your whistle 'Whistle' in this drinking phrase is understood, by some, to refer to the mouth or throat, but there is an earlier, and much more likely, origin to the expression. The Norsemen, noted for their hard-drinking, had whistles fitted to their drinking vessels so that replenishments could be summoned immediately when they were empty.

A story goes that when one of the Danes, a giant of a man with drinking capacity to match, visited Scotland, armed with a whistle by his pot, he boasted that he could drink any man under the table. His confidence was such that he offered his highly-treasured whistle as the prize, and the last man to blow it would be the winner.

He had never lost a contest — but the hardy Scots weren't exactly teetotallers, and amongst his opponents was one who kept drinking continuously for three days and was still able to 'wet the whistle' to summon more drink while the Dane was slumped under the table.

Our's not to reason why is used when an order given by a superior must be obeyed without question, even if one does not understand, or agree with it. When a group of people has been told to do something, or carry out an impossible task, the tension has often been relieved when one of them has remarked, 'Our's not to reason why'. This was particularly appropriate during both World Wars. The phrase originated at the time of the Crimean War (1854–1856), being immortalized in Tennyson's poem *The Charge of the Light Brigade.*

> Their's not to make reply,
> Their's not to reason why,
> Their's but to do and die.

To be given a wigging This comes from the heyday of the wig in the 18th century when, apart from those worn by the fashionable, judges and persons in authority wore huge wigs. These important people were known as 'bigwigs' and 'to be given a wigging' was to receive a scolding, or sharp reprimand, from a bewigged superior. Wigs are still worn in the law courts and by the Speaker of the House of Commons.

Another old phrase: 'There will be wigs on the green' referred to the possibility of two individuals, or a group of people, coming to blows and ending up in a fierce fight.

Win *see* To win in a CANTER

Win *see* To win one's SPURS

To whistle down the wind — To get the wind up — Whistle for it — To take the wind out of one's sails — Get wind of — Something in the wind — Go like the wind — Find out which way the wind blows — Three sheets in the wind — Tempering the wind to the shorn lamb In the days of sailing ships, sailors considered whistling to be unlucky. This was founded on the superstition that whistling, which imitated the sound of the wind, could raise it, as if by magic. Some feared that TO WHISTLE DOWN THE WIND might prove to be too effective, resulting in severe gales, and subsequent shipwreck. Hence the other expression TO GET THE WIND UP, or to be frightened.

On land, the expression TO WHISTLE FOR IT is a sarcastic one, meaning that there is no hope of a person getting what they want and that they can whistle in vain for it.

TO TAKE THE WIND OUT OF ONE'S SAILS, which originated during the 19th century, is also a derogatory phrase, in which one person frustrates another's plans, or anticipates their arguments. (*See* 'To steal someone's THUNDER'.)

To GET WIND OF anything is to suspect that something is about to happen, or to hear a rumour about it. It derives from a hunting term.

SOMETHING IN THE WIND, similarly, means that something is afoot or that something is being prepared, or that steps are being taken, secretly. To GO LIKE THE WIND is to move swiftly, or run like mad when the hunter becomes the hunted, and is being pursued by a wild animal.

By way of contrast, to FIND OUT WHICH WAY THE WIND BLOWS is a mid-16th century expression still in use today by politicians, and others, to find out the state of public opinion — or what developments in some state of affairs are possible or likely.

THREE SHEETS IN THE WIND brings us back to the nautical world, the 'sheet' being the rope or chain at the lower end of a sail used for regulating its tension. A flowing sail is one eased for free wind, and not close-hauled; 'three sheets in the wind' is a popular expression used to describe someone out of control and very drunk.

TEMPERING THE WIND TO THE SHORN LAMB means to make allowances for weaknesses but it has nothing to do with any of the previous sayings and needs some qualification. Laurence Sterne (1713–1768), the British novelist, wrote 'God tempers the wind to the shorn lamb' in his book *A Sentimental Journey* but the phrase was not original, he had merely substituted 'lamb' for 'sheep'. This was poetic licence because lambs are, in fact, never shorn.

To tilt at windmills is an expression which came into everyday language as a result of one of the most famous stories in the world, *Don Quixote*, from the imagination of the great Spanish writer, Miguel de Cervantes, who died on the same day as the greatest English dramatist, William Shakespeare.

Cervantes' work was a satire, written in two parts, published in 1605

[152]

and 1615, on the medieval knights and the romantic days of chivalry, long past, but still influencing people. Don Quixote imagined that those times had returned and that he was a courageous knight errant, full of ideas about honour, and impracticable plans to help others, regardless of his own material interests, safety and welfare. (This sort of behaviour became known as 'Quixotic'.)

During his adventures, Don Quixote's crazed mind leads him to believe that his mission in life is to fight the wrongs of the whole world single-handed. Everything takes on giant proportions in his mind — inns become castles, grazing sheep are transformed into armies, and slaves become worthy gentlemen in need of his assistance.

Don Quixote's most famous feat was to tilt at a group of windmills, which he believed were giants in disguise. With little thought of the fierce and unequal combat likely to ensue, he spurred his old plough-horse full tilt at the first of forty windmills. His lance became tangled in one of the mill's whirling sails, which sent him and his faithful mount tumbling over the ground. Undismayed by such 'trickery', he remounted to set upon further adventures, righting wrongs that seldom existed, or making them worse if they did.

The phrase 'tilting at windmills' is now used to imply the futility or total impracticality of an action.

A good wine needs no bush This saying goes back over 2,000 years to the time when the Bacchanalia, or festival of Bacchus, was celebrated every third year in Rome, until 186 BC. Bacchus was the Roman name for Dionysus, the god of wine, who was always associated with vine leaves or ivy. Most Roman shops had a sign of some sort outside to denote their trade, and the evergreen emblem of ivy, or vine leaves, in the form of a bush, used to be attached to a large pole outside their taverns; the Romans introduced the custom to England.

The proverb arose from the reasoning that it was not necessary to advertise a good wine, with a bush outside the tavern, because everyone would soon get to know about it.

In England, a law was passed by Richard II, in 1393, which made it compulsory for inns to display a sign outside, though it did not apply to other trades.

The phrase is still applied today to goods and provisions of excellent quality to imply that they will speak for themselves.

Wives *see* Old wives' TALES

Wolf *see* Wolf in sheep's CLOTHING

Touch wood Almost everyone, whether superstitious or not, touches wood to attempt to make sure that what they have said, or hoped for, comes into being, or to try to see that a run of good luck will not change, and misfortune will be warded off. Usually they touch any wooden object that happens to be handy, but if there is no wood around they just say 'touch wood'.

The custom is of ancient origin, from the times when trees were believed to contain guardian spirits, and to touch the tree was a way of paying respect to the spirits, as well as making an appeal for good fortune.

The trees considered sacred, having protective powers, were the oak, above all, and the apple, ash, hawthorn, hazel and willow. Nowadays, we tend to touch any wood, without enquiring which type of tree it comes from.

Words *see* TO BANDY words

Work *see* To work like a NAVVY

Index

[161]